CREOLE COOKING

W9-AZA-595

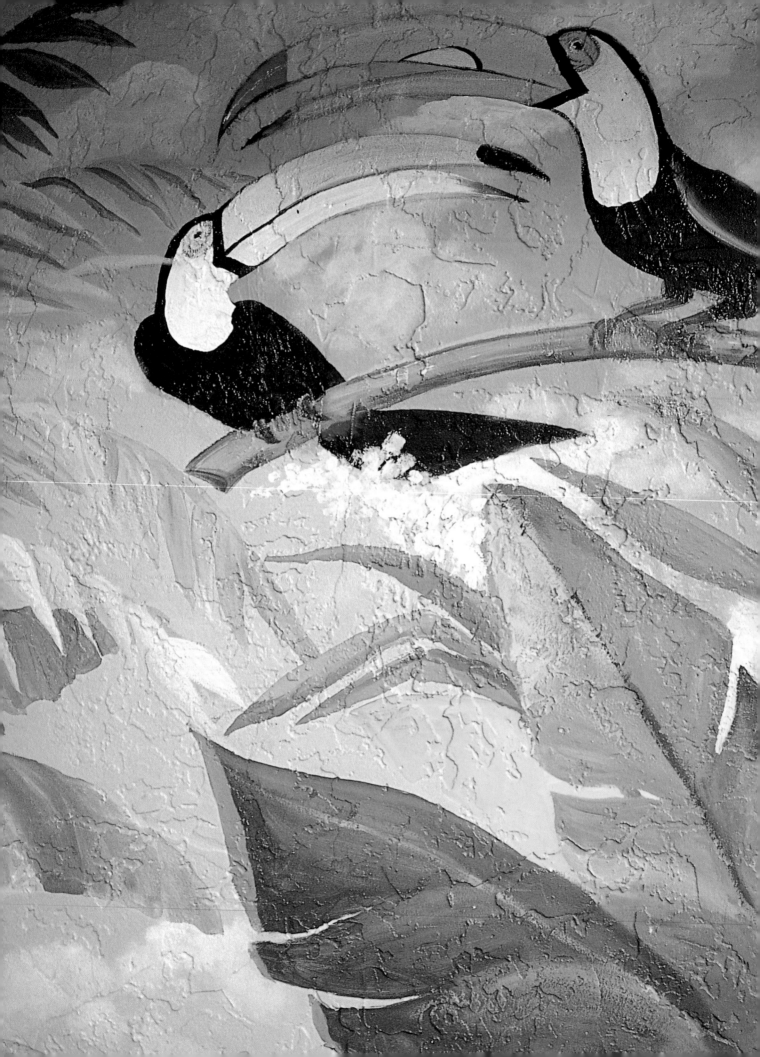

CREOLE COOKING

SUE MULLIN

THE TASTE OF TROPICAL ISLANDS

CHARTWELL
BOOKS, INC.

A QUINTET BOOK

Published by Chartwell Books
A Division of Book Sales, Inc.
114 Northfield Avenue
Edison, New Jersey 08837

This edition produced for sale in the U.S.A., its
territories and dependencies only.

First paperback edition published 1996.

Copyright © 1993 Quintet Publishing Limited.
All rights reserved. No part of this publication
may be reproduced, stored in a retrieval system
or transmitted in any form or by any means,
electronic, mechanical, photocopying,
recording or otherwise, without the permission
of the copyright holder.

ISBN 0-7858-0646-6

This book was designed and produced by
Quintet Publishing Limited
6 Blundell Street
London N7 9BH

Creative Director: Richard Dewing
Designer: Suzie Hooper
Project Editor: Stefanie Foster
Editor: Diana Vowles
Home Economy: Judith Kelsey
Photographer: Trevor Wood

Typeset in Great Britain by
Central Southern Typesetters, Eastbourne
Manufactured in Singapore by
Bright Arts Pte. Ltd
Printed in Hong Kong by
Sing Cheong Printing Co. Ltd.

CONTENTS

INTRODUCTION

WHILE IT HAS been developed and refined over a period of 500 years, Creole cuisine has been slow to make the voyage beyond the shores of the hundreds of islands that make up the West Indies. It seems that the exotic and piquant cooking of the Caribbean has spread in the leisurely, old-fashioned way: person-to-person, island-to-island, and, finally, hemisphere-to-hemisphere.

This last transmigration is due in part to tourism. Anyone taking a Caribbean holiday invariably goes home with fond memories of the island's delicacies, from finger foods sold from seaside shacks to sophisticated dishes served in smart resort hotels and inns on fine china gloriously garnished with hibiscus. Fortunately, reproducing much of this exciting cuisine far from the islands is becoming quite easy, thanks to the rapid growth in exports of exotic fruit and vegetables, and the demand for these products created by communities of West Indians in many parts of the world. Such enclaves are sizable and the interest in Caribbean culture and cuisine even greater, judging by the rapid growth of West Indian carnivals on two continents. At the last count, Great Britain hosted 18 West Indian carnivals per year, and Toronto is the site of a huge annual extravaganza called Caribana, which draws more than 3000 participants, and 200,000 spectators.

Food may be a simple pleasure, but in the islands the emphasis is indeed on the pleasure. Eating is called the favorite indoor sport of the Caribbean, and even island music takes its cue from cuisine. Whole musical rhythms and dances are named for foods: *salsa*, for example, and *merengue*. There are songs about the virtues of wine-braised goat and fried green plantains, and rhymes for children to learn their letters by that cite an island foodstuff or dish for almost every letter, for example "A fi ackee, saltfish bes' frien', an' B fi bammy, banana an' den . . . ," and so on through the alphabet.

THE FIRST WEST INDIANS

The cuisine of the islands, one of the most diverse on earth, owes much to the indigenous Amerindians. For centuries before Columbus arrived, a tribe called the Arawak was growing garlic, hot peppers, tobacco, corn, cotton, papaya, guava, mamey, pineapples, and cassava, and grinding the berries, buds, and leaves of trees and plants to make spices. They concocted a preservative from cassava and cooked a meat and hot pepper stew which, under the name of pepperpot, is still eaten today throughout the islands. They were also barbecueing food over aromatic wood fires and making popcorn. Even the word barbecue – or, in Spanish, *barbacoa* – comes from the Taino tribe of Arawaks who once peopled Haiti. Some food historians say that tomatoes also made their way from Mexico to the islands in pre-Columbian days, and possibly other foodstuffs such as bell peppers, squash, and chocolate; one of the first New World foodstuffs Columbus presented to Queen Isabella of Spain was the Caribbean sweet potato, a boniato. (It was called a potato because the Arawak word for it, *batata,* sounded like "potato.") White potatoes did not arrive in Europe until later, and they came from the cooler mountain climes of South America.

Another item Columbus took back with him wasn't quite the overnight hit boniatos were, but their popularity over time is unprecedented. Within a century of Columbus' first voyage, chili peppers were to be found throughout Asia, and they have since become one of the most widely used spices in the world. India leads all nations today in per capita consumption and in 1991 chili-spiked salsa overtook sweet tomato ketchup as the USA's top condiment.

THE AFRICAN CONNECTION

While the Arawaks were killed off by other Indians, (mainly the warlike Caribs) and by white men's diseases and brutality, another group of people brought to the islands their own cooking techniques and food tastes, and incorporated them with the beautiful fruits and homely tubers of the Amerindian diet. These people were slaves from the west coast of Africa, shipped in their thousands to the islands in the 17th century to work the sugar cane plantations. A number of roots and seeds from the west coast were brought to the islands along with the slaves, and soon the West Indies was flourishing with pigeon peas, black-eyed peas, okra, and greens such as the leaves of the taro plant called callaloo.

With the vast species of fish and crustaceans teeming in the seas of the Caribbean – pompano, grouper, marlin, tuna, amberjack, mullet, flying fish, kingfish, dolphin, snapper, lobster, crab, shrimp, conch, spiny lobster, and barracuda, to name just a few – seafood is another hallmark of Caribbean food. Beef dishes are of more recent origin, and many of the recipes in this book are adapted from ones used for wild game and pork.

Carnival time in the Caribbean.

COLONIAL AND OTHER INFLUENCES

Over time, dishes made their way between the islands with surprisingly few changes on the way, except that they might gain a new title in the language of whichever colonial power governed the island. Although other races brought their various influences to bear, the foundation of island cuisine is Afro-Amerindian. Creole, then, is a bit of a misnomer, for this is not a cuisine created by people born in the West Indies of European descent, the dictionary definition of Creole.

This is not to say that Europeans did not have a profound effect on island cuisine. Of the many European groups colonizing the islands, the Spanish, French, and British were the largest and most influential – the Spanish by introducing the islanders to cabbage, onions, and sugar cane, and the French by bringing chives, and by teaching sophisticated cooking techniques, such as poaching fish in spices and peppers. And all three groups bequeathed a taste for salted cod which still survives in the islands today.

From Spain there also came Seville oranges, which the Dutch later used on their island of Curaçao to make the liqueur of the same name, and most food historians credit the Spanish too for the islands' sweet orange, lime and banana trees. The British naval captain William Bligh, after the Mutiny on the HMS *Bounty*, sailed a second time to Tahiti, and thence to Jamaica with a shipload of Tahitian breadfruits intended to nourish slaves on the island. It seems, though, that the slaves refused to eat the musky,

The Caribbean islands remain some of the most idyllic spots on earth.

Island specialty.

doughy fruits, and fed them to the animals instead. Another fruit Captain Bligh introduced fared better – the *Blighia sapida*, named for the captain, but commonly called ackee. Today, ackee and saltfish is sometimes regarded as Jamaica's national dish.

The British also introduced blood sausage, Worcestershire sauce, and rum. Even the word "rum" is English, and tellingly comes from rumbullion, meaning a great disturbance. Nowadays, not just drinks but tasty dishes are imbued with demon rum, made from the juice of the tall sugar cane plants which sway to and fro throughout the islands and are said to have originally been planted by Christopher Columbus himself upon his second voyage to the West Indies. A tamer beverage Britain introduced to the islands via Grenada, Barbados, and the Bahamas, was tea.

Subsequent immigrant groups have left their marks as well. On Sint Maarten, Aruba and Curaçao, you'll find East Indian rijsttafels, a delicious legacy of Indonesian immigrants to those Dutch islands. And on Trinidad, captivating curries have been prepared in homes and restaurants since 1834 when enormous numbers of Hindus, Moslems and Parsees flocked to the British-held island. It is no accident that on the streets of Port of Spain today, you see a roti cart on just about every street corner – Indians today make up about half the population. This pattern of immigration continued into the 19th century on many of the islands, including the French-held ones, such as Martinique, and Guadeloupe, where a "national" dish called colombo, actually a curry, was introduced by Hindu workers from Bengal.

SOME LIKE IT HOT

Despite so many influences from such far-flung parts of the world West Indians share a love for many of the same dishes and, while one island's dish might be more spicy or have a different texture than the next island's, basic ingredients remain the same. Cubans favor black beans while most other islanders prefer red beans, for example. Virgin Islanders like to use spinach instead of callaloo in the soup of the same name, but other islanders insist on genuine callaloo, the leaves of the taro plant. Cooks in the Bahamas have long been famous for their raised bread, whereas Cubans like their raised bread toasted and slathered with garlic and butter, Trinidadians favor East Indian-style parathas called roti, and Bajans are likely to opt for bread that we might call a fruit cake, replete with boniatos, coconut, fruits, spices, and rum.

You could take a crash-course in the history of the islands by studying just one plant, the hot pepper. In Jamaica, for example, escaped slaves used them to help preserve food in the hot, humid areas in which they were hiding. Later, on islands stretching from Trinidad and Tobago to Martinique and Guadeloupe, Hindu workers from Bengal brought their cooking skills to bear on tough cuts of meat, such as goat, and added the local hot peppers to their marinades. On these and neighboring islands, hot peppers became an essential ingredient in many dishes. On the other hand, in Cuba – where the *Habañero* (which translates as "Havana-like") is believed to have originated – hot peppers are seldom grown or eaten. They were suspected by the Spanish colonists of making animals sick.

Many inhabitants in the West Indies can trace their roots directly to tribes in Africa, such as the Haitians whose ancestors lived in Dahomey (now Benin), a small country in West Africa. And it is this same West

African influence that is seen in the United States in a few Cajun-Creole dishes, particularly okra-thickened gumbo; French refugees fleeing the slave uprisings in Saint-Domingue in the 1790s, which culminated in the establishment of the independent state of Haiti, came to New Orleans with their own household slaves, including cooks, in tow.

Do not confuse the Creole of the islands with Cajun-Creole dishes. The influences of Acadia and Alsace-Lorraine so prominent in many dishes of Louisiana and the Gulf States are not a factor in the islands because of a different ethnic history. Island Creole cooking uses a lot more peppers, tomatoes, tomato paste, lard, tropical tubers, fruit, and spices such as allspice, cinnamon, clove, ginger, and nutmeg than Cajun-Creole and less butter, cream, celery, basil, and the gravy-like mixture of oil or butter and flour called *roux*. Cajun-Creole gumbo – *gombo* is the African word for okra so there's no question of the dish's origin – can even be made without okra! They still call the dish a gumbo – filé gumbo, to be precise – and it is thickened with filé powder, which is made from the leaves of the sassafras tree, rather than gumbo.

Like Caribbean cooking, carnival is colorful and exuberant.

THE SECOND DISCOVERY OF THE NEW WORLD

In the West Indies, it seems that the New World is being discovered all over again. Accomplished chefs from around the world and from the islands themselves have chosen to live and work on their own little piece of paradise, bringing *haute cuisine* to the Caribbean. When you visit the islands next time, don't be surprised if you find dishes such as iguana *au vin*, and avocado ice cream on the menu.

So it is that I have tried to include here some of the more feasible – in terms of availability of ingredients – traditional dishes of the islands, but also sophisticated dishes inspired by those new explorers, the chefs who have adopted the islands and been inspired by the tropical fruit, tubers, and spices.

I have skipped over recipes for roasted wild goat, raccoon, sea urchin, and manicou, a possum stew delicacy in Trinidad. And I hope purists will forgive me for passing over mannish water, a soup made from goat offal. Many of those ingredients are hard to come by in the Caribbean Gateway City of Miami, let alone more distant parts of the world. Luckily, Caribbean cuisine gets its unique spirit from spice blends and marinades whose ingredients are easy to find, easy to put together, and easy to eat – especially when capped off with a daiquiri, planter's punch or a cup of the best coffee in the world, Jamaican Blue Mountain.

READY, SET, COOK

HOT PEPPERS

The hot peppers of the Caribbean are the *habañeros*, also known as country peppers or bird peppers – this last because even the birds in the islands have developed a taste for fiery cuisine and nibble on them. In the Bahamas, they are called Bahama Mama. Another amusing English name for them is Scotch Bonnet – because, it is said, the bottom looks like a tam o'shanter. They start out green but are red, orange, yellow, or white when ripe, and about the size of Italian plum tomatoes. These are among the hottest peppers in the world – *jalapeños* rank 5 on the Heat Scale, but *habañeros* are 10 or twice as hot – and they are used in all island condiments (see below), in many sauces, rubs, curries, and marinades, and in other dishes such as salads, soups, stews, and fritters.

You may substitute any hot pepper you like in these recipes; fresh ones provide the best crunchy texture and vivid color. But please wear rubber gloves when handling peppers and do taste a tiny bit before deciding how much heat you want in the dish you're preparing. Use the measurements in these recipes as just one cook's suggestion; like perfume, each and every hot pepper – even those in the same "family" – has its own essence and is likely to react differently on you than on me. And, whatever you do, keep your hands away from your face. I inadvertently touched my eye once when I was a young girl helping my mother can hot peppers, and the sting was so sharp I thought I was blinded. You'll find several hot pepper sauce recipes in the section on Jerked Dishes (page 81). You may substitute a bottled sauce, such as the ones listed below, or Tabasco or a similar hot sauce if you prefer. Whatever sauce you're using to prepare a dish, remember to place a bowl or bottle of it on the table for dousing purposes, as is the custom in the islands.

COMMERCIALLY PREPARED CONDIMENTS

Several types of prepared sauces are exported from the Caribbean islands. The brand names of many of them warn you of their most noteworthy characteristic: Jamaica Hell-Fire, Bonney Pepper Sauce, Doc's Special Jamaica Hellfire, Evadney's Jamaican Hot Sauce, Pepper Sherry Sauce, Hell In A Bottle, Pickapeppa, Matouk's Hot Calypso Sauce, MP West Indian Hot Flambeau, Trinidad Pepper Sauce, West Indies Creole Hot Pepper Sauce, and Melinda's XXXtra Hot Sauce.

Jerk marinades and curry powders are also canned and exported. Labels include Vernon's Jamaican Jerk Sauce, Walkerswood Jerk Seasoning, Uncle Bum's Jamaican Marinade, and Hot Jamaican Curry Powder.

JERK MAGIC

Long before Columbus arrived in the Caribbean islands, the Arawak Indians were preserving meat by rubbing spices and acidic hot peppers into strips of it, and then cooking it slowly over an aromatic wood fire until it was bone dry but still flavorful. Later, African slaves in Jamaica adopted the technique when they escaped from their captors and hid in the mountains. It was a variation, after all, of an African technique of cutting game meat into chunks, preparing it to ward off flies, and laying it in the sun to dry. The strips of meat the Maroons, as they were called, smoked in the mountains held up well in the soggy humidity of the tropics, and the tradition took firm hold. Early North American trappers, traders, and explorers would likewise learn the preservation technique from the North American Indians. Later, when pioneers pushed westward into lands populated by Mexicans and Western Indians, they coined the word "jerky" for the dried strips of meat that kept them alive during their long journeys. The words jerk and jerky come from the English corruption of *charqui*, a Spanish word which the conquistadors, in turn, got from the Quechua Indians of Peru and Ecuador. (Linguists point out that *escharqui* is what the Indians called it, but the Spanish dropped the first syllable.)

From the survivalist beginnings of jerky in the States there developed a tradition of delicious chargrilled steaks and smoked hams, while in Jamaica, Barbados, Trinidad, Tobago, and other islands of the West Indies an entire culinary art form grew up around jerk. With the advent of refrigeration and modern food processing the need to preserve meat by drying disappeared, but the taste for spiciness and the tenderizing benefits of marinades, pastes, and rubs did not. Today we can cook jerk dishes in a variety of ways, but the early method of slowly grilling and smoking meats over an aromatic pimento (allspice) or guava wood fire is still practiced. This style of cooking is widespread throughout the Caribbean – in Jamaica, for example, jerk barbecue shacks or pits dot the entire island. The fellow who prepares the meat, poultry, fish, or seafood is called the "jerk mon."

There are many jerk seasoning combinations in the islands today. Most call for a combination of island spices, such as allspice, cinnamon, and nutmeg, plus hot peppers – dry, liquid, or chopped whole – and onion and garlic in some form. Some jerks incorporate acidic liquids such as lime juice or vinegar to add tartness; some include ingredients such as sugar or molasses to add sweetness. And some are very complex, combining all the aforementioned plus herbs, condiments such as Worcestershire sauce, soy sauce, and mustard, and other enhancers from chicken stock to rum.

FRUITS, SQUASHES AND TUBERS

BONIATO A white-fleshed tuber, this is a particular type of tropical sweet potato. It has a smooth texture when cooked and is only slightly sweet. Try to buy small boniato because they're more tender. If you cannot find these, use sweet, or white regular, potatoes.

CALABAZA This large squash the size of a soccer ball with orange flesh is usually sold in wedges that look like pieces of pumpkin, although the texture and flavor of calabaza is somewhat sweeter. You can usually find this squash in West Indian grocers and market stalls. Hubbard or butternut squashes make good substitutes.

CASSAVA This large, starchy tuber (also called yuca and manioc) is used in African, Caribbean and Latin American cooking, and is available at West Indian grocers and market stalls. Tapioca is made from the starch from the root. Not to be confused with bitter cassava (which is toxic unless cooked and is used in poison darts), nor with yucca, the desert plant that sprouts ivory-colored flowers. Far from pretty, the skin of cassava is bark-like and the flesh inside is as hard as a brick. It is not the easiest thing to work with considering it also has a fibrous cord running through it, but for those who persist, the reward is a tasty tuber that seems to suck up the rich and spicy flavors of Caribbean cuisine. If you can't find cassava, you can substitute white potatoes.

CHAYOTE Also called christophene, cho-cho, and chu-chu, this is a tropical squash-like fruit that resembles a green gnarled pear. It must be cooked and has a slightly citrus tang and a taste of cucumbers. Chayote keeps well, seldom losing its crunchy texture, and is available at many specialty shops and market stalls year-round.

COCONUT MILK, CREAM, & FLAKES Not to be confused with the juice inside the fresh fruit, coconut milk is made by soaking dried, unsweetened coconut in boiling water, emulsifying it in a food processor or blender, and then straining it – 2 cups water to 1 cup coconut makes milk and 1 cup water to 1 cup coconut makes cream. Canned sweetened coconut milk, which is great for tropical drinks, is sold in Asian and Caribbean grocers. You can make your own sweetened coconut milk by steeping 2 tbsp. sweetened coconut flakes in water for 5 minutes. To toast flaked coconut, place a skillet over medium-high heat, add the coconut flakes and cook for 5 to 6 minutes, stirring frequently, until golden. Unsweetened coconut flakes are also available.

GUAVA Grown in Australia, South Africa and some parts of South-East Asia as well as in the Caribbean, this walnut- to apple-sized fruit tastes like straw-berries to some, bananas to others, pineapple to still others and like nothing else in the world to the rest of us. It's ripe and sweet when it feels like a ripe pear.

MALANGA Another starchy tuber with bark-like skin, this one is also used as a Caribbean potato and has an intriguing nutty flavor.

MAMAY SAPOTE The sapote family is huge, but Cubans will immediately tell you that there is only one worth considering! The national fruit of the island has a rough, brownish skin, glorious, grainy, salmon-colored fruit inside, and a glistening black pit. The taste hints of peaches, cinnamon, and pumpkin.

MANGO This fruit from a tropical evergreen tree is about the size of an orange and has juicy yellow-orange pulp. Mangoes are harvested in the Caribbean throughout the summer, and can be found canned. Most of the world's many types turn from green to variegated shades of yellow, orange, and red when ripe; the small Asian varieties are said to be the best. Squeeze lightly to make sure the fruit is not hard and unripe. Some people are allergic to the juice of the mango, and their skin will swell or blister upon touching it. Wear rubber gloves if you're concerned about this. There is no perfect substitute, but you could try a combination of the flavors in mango: peaches, pineapples, and apricots. Some people also like to substitute nectarines.

PAPAYAS Also known as fruta bomba and pawpaw, papayas are abundant throughout the Caribbean. They come in myriad shapes and colors, and are about the size of avocados. The flesh ranges from pale yellow to golden orange when ripe, and the fruit is available year-round. Green-fleshed, unripe papayas can be cooked like squash; ripe ones are used in fruit salads or dressings, or poached for desserts. If you wish to ripen one, place it in a thick paper bag, perforated with a few holes; after several days at room temperature it will ripen to a rosy yellowish hue. The papaya has delicious black seeds that taste like watercress and can be used in a salad or vinaigrette. Papaya – like mango – has an abrasive sap, so put on the gloves.

PASSION FRUIT Unattractive on the outside, this brownish-skinned fruit the size of a large egg has unusual pulp that tastes like a combination of lemons, pineapples, and guavas.

PLANTAIN A starchy member of the banana family, the plantain must be cooked. The flesh can be ivory, yellow, or pink. If the recipe calls for green plantains, your task is straightforward: look for green-skinned plantains. These are starchy and not sweet. If ripe plantains are specified, look for ones that are turning from green to yellow-brown. If all you can find are green-skinned ones and your recipe calls for ripened, place them in an oven set at 300°F until the skin turns black and begins to split.

SEVILLE ORANGE JUICE This is the juice of the Seville or bitter orange, usually available at Hispanic markets. Brought to the islands by the Spanish, the trees bear fruit whose pulp is too acidic to eat. However, the juice is widely used in marinades on the Spanish-speaking islands and in the liqueur Curaçao. Seville oranges are also used to make marmalade. Mix one part naturally sweet orange with one part lime or lemon juice to make a substitute.

STARFRUIT This yellow, waxy fruit looks something like an accordion-pleated, squat banana. When it is cut across, the slices look like yellow stars – hence its name. In season in January, these little beauties provide a fresh fragrance and a sweet and tart flavor that adds zest to dishes. You can eat these "stars" as they are without peeling them or simply slice them to make a pretty garnish. White-skinned varieties generally taste sweet, like a combination of plums, apples, grapes, and a hint of lemon. Yellow-skinned ones are usually a little tart in flavor if they have very narrow ribs.

PULSES

BEANS It is not always necessary to soak dry beans these days since some have been pre-processed – check the directions on the package. If you don't have the correct beans for the recipe to hand, simply substitute whatever beans you do have; most recipes work with any kind and only purists would find fault. Just remember that wine, citrus juice, vinegar, and tomatoes contain acids which will prevent beans from softening properly, so add these ingredients, if called for, when the beans are almost done.

BLACK-EYED PEAS These pea-like seeds come from the pods of a tropical vine that grows in the Caribbean. Also called cowpeas or black-eyed beans, they are neither peas nor beans but lentils. Again, read the package as to whether to soak or not. Cook black-eyed peas in the same water they have soaked in, and fewer nutrients will leach out. To prevent the peas from splitting open, simmer them slowly.

PIGEON PEAS Of African origin, these round seeds the size of small garden peas are also known as gunga or gungo peas, arhar dah, channa peas, gandules (in Spanish), goongoo, green peas, congo peas, and tropical green peas. Dried or fresh, they are very popular in West Indian cooking. You can find these in Asian and West Indian grocers. Red beans may be substituted.

AROMATIC SPICES OF THE WEST INDIES

So many wonderful spices come from the West Indies – cinnamon, cloves, nutmeg, mace, ginger, allspice – it's hard to know where to begin. For the most part, these are familiar items to cooks everywhere so they don't require description. I'm sure, though, that you'll find the combinations of spices in these recipes for hot pepper sauces, marinades, jerk seasonings, colombos, and curries exciting. Of course, food tastes dramatically better if you use fresh herbs and spices. For the next best thing, try to buy the berries, buds, leaves or seeds whole, in small quantities, and crumble leaves by hand or with a rolling pin, and grind seeds and berries in a spice mill or food processor. Keep the red ones in tight-fitting jars in the refrigerator to prevent oxidation.

ALLSPICE Also known as pimento and Jamaican pepper, allspice comes from the Caribbean and is a mainstay of local dishes. It is not, as one might suspect, a blend of other spices. While it does hint of cinnamon, cloves, nutmeg, and pepper, it's actually an individual spice, the dried berry of the pimento tree, which is not to be confused with pimiento, the tiny, mild peppers used to stuff olives. While others have been hard put to know what to do with allspice other than use it in spice cake, West Indians use the berry in myriad dishes. (They also use the aromatic pimento wood in barbecues.) Do make room in your spice cabinet for allspice berries or, if these are not available, allspice powder to add pizzazz to mild-flavored foods such as turnips, sweet potatoes, eggplant, beet, beans, and beef, and enhance boniato's subtle spicy taste.

CILANTRO Also called Chinese parsley, Mexican parsley or coriander, this herb has a broad, flat, serrated leaf. There really is no substitute for its sharp flavor, although some cooks like to use flat-leaved parsley, which looks but does not taste similar. Most Caribbean dishes have plenty of spicing, so I suggest you just leave cilantro out if you don't like it. Don't confuse fresh cilantro with ground coriander, which is from the seed of the plant and has a different taste altogether – and steer away from commercial dried cilantro, which can taste like acrid tobacco.

TAMARIND The fruit of this tree with fern-like branches comes in long, seed-studded pods that look like gigantic brown peapods. The tangy brown pulp inside is edible and is used in Indian, Oriental, and Latin American cooking, as well as Caribbean. Frozen or dried pulp is available in grocery shops catering to those ethnic groups. Tamarind may be eaten as a fresh fruit, rolled in granulated sugar to make a sweetmeat or mixed with water and sugar to make a drink Spanish-speaking people call a *refresco*. In recipes that call for tamarind juice, simply simmer ½ cup of crumbled dried tamarind with 1½ cups water in a heavy small saucepan for 10 minutes. Remove from the heat and leave to stand for an hour, then strain through a fine sieve into a small bowl. It should be the consistency of heavy cream. If too thick, thin it with a little more water. Although you may not have realized it, you have probably been eating tamarind for years – it's one of the ingredients in Worcestershire sauce.

VANILLA Vanilla was unknown to European cooks until the 16th century. The fruit of a tropical orchid, vanilla beans are cured and fermented to produce the volatile oil vanillin, which gives the characteristic aroma and flavor – sweet, spicy, and slightly woody, with a nuance of chocolate. (It is this nuance that makes white chocolate taste like chocolate even though it has no chocolate in it!) Some of these recipes call for the optional use of whole vanilla beans, which are not easily found in many places. If you do find them, however, they add something quite elegant and complex to the dish. You can use up any leftover pieces by making your own extract – simply combine 1 cup brandy and two vanilla beans cut into 2 inch pieces in a jar with a tight lid. Cover and leave to stand for 3 months, shaking weekly. Artificial vanilla extract may be substituted.

CHORIZO The Spanish brought their love of spicy, lightly smoked pork sausage to the islands. If you cannot find it at a delicatessen, you can substitute Italian sausage.

CONCH The meat from this large, 12 inch long mollusc is tough but is pounded and used in many island dishes. The Carib word for it is lambi, which is used on some of the islands, while others call it concha or conch. This last is pronounced as "conk" (like the French *conque*). In the recipe in this book, it is best to substitute squid or clams.

GHEE Because of the East Indian influence on Creole cuisine, ghee is called for in some recipes. Also called clarified butter, ghee is simply butter that has the milk solids removed so that it can tolerate high temperatures without burning. You can buy ghee at Asian and West Indian groceries; to make it yourself, place the butter in a heavy pan over low heat. As the butter melts and white solids curdle on the surface, pour into a glass pitcher. After a few minutes the butter will separate into layers with the milk solids on the bottom. At this point, strain the clear yellow top layer into a lidded container. Ghee will keep for weeks in the refrigerator, and it can also be frozen.

A FEW WORDS ABOUT EQUIPMENT

No extraordinary equipment is needed – after all, West Indians have been cooking for many years in what many people would consider to be primitive conditions. A word of warning about bowls, pots, pans and the like: many Creole dishes contain acids such as lime juice and vinegar, so use non-reactive cookware to prevent pitting. If you're short on glass mixing bowls, big, strong, sealable plastic bags are excellent containers for liquidy marinated foods that must be refrigerated. If you need to turn the food occasionally, nothing could be easier than flipping the bag over in the fridge.

DRINKS

MANY COCKTAIL recipes call for sugar syrup. This is easy — boil 1 part water to 2 parts sugar for 5 minutes. Make a batch and keep it in the refrigerator for the next time you're thirsty for a taste of the West Indies.

Crushed ice is another common ingredient in these drinks. If you're planning to serve them regularly, an ice crusher — either manually operated or an electric model — is a wise investment. (If you own a food processor check the instruction booklet first to see if it's possible to do the job in that expensive bit of equipment.) If all else fails, wrap ice cubes in a clean towel and smash them with a hammer or, if you have a very hard floor, buy ice in a heavy plastic bag and then bang the bag against the floor.

Rum is, of course, the liquor of choice in the land of the sugar cane, but there is a world of difference between the dry rums of, say, Puerto Rico and Cuba, and the rums of Jamaica — and there are differences between the rums of Jamaica and those of Barbados, Haiti, and Martinique. These variations arise according to which product of sugar cane is used to make the rum and the method of distillation. In these recipes, though, a light rum is generally called for in the citrusy drinks, and a dark rum for sweeter and spicier fire in the belly.

Except for beautiful fresh tropical fruit, most of the ingredients in these drinks are fairly common to any well-stocked bar. Do experiment with the wide variety of rums from the islands — quite a few are bottled in miniatures — and check the frozen food and fruit juice sections of your supermarket. Many exciting nectars and juice concentrates made from exotic tropical fruits are coming onto the market.

If you're thirsty for a non-alcoholic but refreshing tropical drink, you'll find plenty of delicious prospects in Punches, Smoothies, & So Forth (page 25).

A PALETTE OF DAIQUIRIS

There are a number of legends surrounding the origins of the daiquiri, most of them very long and involved. One holds that the recipe was secret and only divulged as part of an initiation rite for a group of American officers setting up Guantanamo Naval Station on Guantanamo Bay in Cuba. Bacardi, one of the world's foremost makers of rum and a firm that started out in Cuba, doesn't pin it down that specifically, but has stated in some of its promotional material that the drink was invented in 1896 by an American mining engineer working at the Daiquiri copper mines. Today, while few people have ever heard of the mine, everyone knows the wonderful drink.

CLASSIC DAIQUIRI

SERVES I

1/4 cup dry, light-bodied rum
1 tsp. sugar syrup
1 1/2 fl. oz. fresh lime juice
Grenadine to taste (optional)

Combine the ingredients in a drink shaker, blender, or food processor, adding Grenadine if liked for a little more sweetness. Serve over crushed ice in a chilled glass.

STRAWBERRIES 'N' ICE CREAM DAIQUIRI

SERVES 2

If you cannot find frozen pink lemonade concentrate, the same effect can be achieved by adding a drop of red food coloring to a normal frozen lemonade concentrate.

1/2 cup dry, light-bodied rum
1 cup crushed ice
1 cup sliced fresh strawberries
1/3 cup frozen pink lemonade concentrate, thawed
1 pint vanilla ice cream

Combine the ingredients in a drink shaker, blender, or food processor. Serve in chilled glasses.

PEACH DAIQUIRI

SERVES 4

1 cup dry, light-bodied rum
2 medium-ripe peaches, pared and pitted, or whole
canned peaches, drained thoroughly and patted dry
with paper towels
1 medium banana
³/4 cup lemon-lime bottled soda
1 tsp. honey
¹/2 tsp. vanilla extract
¹/4 tsp. ground cinnamon
1–2 cups crushed ice
peach slices, to garnish (optional)

Blend the rum, peaches, banana, lemon-lime soda, honey, vanilla extract, and cinnamon in a blender or food processor. Add ¹/2 cup ice and blend until the mixture is smooth. Pour into four glasses, adding more ice if desired. Garnish with peach slices.

STRAWBERRY-BANANA DAIQUIRI

SERVES 3

1 cup dry, light-bodied rum
1 pint fresh strawberries, hulled
1 large banana
³/4 cup frozen limeade concentrate
2¹/4 tbsp. fresh lime juice

Blend the ingredients in a blender or food processor until the mixture is smooth. Add ice cubes and blend the drink for a few seconds until it is slushy. Serve in chilled glasses.

PASSIONATE BANANA DAIQUIRI

SERVES 3

3 fl. oz. dry, light-bodied rum
1 ripe banana
¼ cup passion fruit juice or canned nectar
1 fl. oz. frozen orange juice concentrate
3 cups crushed ice
3 orange slices, to garnish

In a blender or food processor, combine the rum, banana, passion fruit juice or nectar, orange juice concentrate, and half the crushed ice, and blend until the mixture is smooth. Pour into three glasses, adding more ice if desired. Garnish each with an orange slice.

COCKTAILS, TODDIES & PARTY FARE

VICE-PRESIDENTE

SERVES 1

This is a version of the Presidente below.

1 fl. oz. dry, light-bodied rum, chilled
1 fl. oz. dry vermouth, chilled
dash of Grenadine

Combine the ingredients in a drink shaker, blender, or food processor and serve in a chilled glass.

PRESIDENTE COCKTAIL

SERVES 1

This is a popular cocktail served throughout the Spanish-speaking islands, named, perhaps, for the president of a yacht club! These smart watering holes perch on many bays in the Caribbean.

1½ fl. oz. dry, light-bodied rum, chilled
1 tsp. dry vermouth, chilled
1 tsp. lemon or lime juice
dash of Grenadine
dash of Curaçao

Combine the ingredients in a drink shaker, blender, or food processor and serve in a chilled glass.

PORT ROYAL

SERVES 1

It is said that a church bell that was hurled into the ocean during a storm off Port Royal peals each time someone downs one of these bell-ringing drinks.

1½ fl. oz. dark Jamaican-style rum
1½ fl. oz. Tia Maria
1 tsp. lime juice

Pour the ingredients into a chilled glass, stir, and serve.

MOJITO

SERVES 1

The word mojito means "soul", and if ever a drink had spirit, this is it.

2 ice cubes
juice of 1 lime
2 drops Angostura bitters
¼ cup dry, light-bodied rum
splash of bottled mineral water
1 fresh mint leaf, to garnish

Place the ice cubes in a tall, chilled glass and add the lime juice, bitters, rum, and mineral water. Stir once, garnish with the mint leaf and serve.

Greatfruit Grapefruit

GREATFRUIT GRAPEFRUIT

SERVES 2

The noble grapefruit is overlooked in cocktails. Here's one that proves it to be a natural.

½ grapefruit, peeled and seeded
1 cup orange juice
¼ cup orange-based liqueur
¼ cup light rum (optional)

Purée the grapefruit in a blender or food processor. Add the orange juice, liqueur, and, if desired, rum. Serve over crushed ice in a chilled glass.

PERFUMED HOLIDAY RUM

SERVES A ROOM FULL OF REVELLERS

This is a wonderful drink to prepare for Christmas.

2 pints dark Jamaican-style rum
4–5 whole cloves
2 allspice berries
1–2 anise seeds
1 whole vanilla bean
1 cinnamon stick

Add all the spices to the bottle of rum and store, capped, for 30 days before drinking. Turn the bottle occasionally to disperse the aromatic spices.

HOT BUTTERED RUM

SERVES 1

This one is an old favorite.

1 tsp. dark brown sugar
½ tsp. unsalted butter, softened
1½ fl. oz. dark Jamaican-style rum
4 whole cloves

Place the sugar in the bottom of a heavy, heatproof 8 fl. oz. mug and dissolve with a few drops of boiling water. Immediately stir the butter into the sugar water with a spoon, then add the rum and cloves. Leave the spoon in the mug and fill with hot water.

HAVANA YACHT CLUB COCKTAIL

SERVES 1

¼ cup dry, light-bodied rum
1 fl. oz. sweet vermouth
dash of apricot brandy
twist of orange rind, to garnish

Combine the ingredients in a drink shaker, blender, or food processor, and serve in a chilled glass garnished with a twist of orange rind.

Havana Yacht Club Cocktail

A COLLECTION OF COLADAS

PIÑA COLADA

SERVES 1

This internationally known drink was invented in Puerto Rico.

1 oz. cream of coconut
¼ cup unsweetened pineapple juice
1 fl. oz. heavy cream
¼ cup light or dark rum
1 cup crushed ice

Mix the cream of coconut, pineapple juice, cream, rum, and half the crushed ice in a drink shaker, blender or food processor. Serve immediately in a chilled glass over the rest of the crushed ice.

BANANA COLADA

SERVES 1

1 oz. cream of coconut
½ ripe banana
¼ cup light or dark rum
1 cup crushed ice

Combine the cream of coconut, banana, rum, and half the crushed ice in a drink shaker, blender, or food processor. Serve immediately in a chilled glass over the remaining crushed ice.

STRAWBERRY COLADA

SERVES 1

1 oz. cream of coconut
6 frozen and thawed or fresh hulled strawberries
¼ cup light or dark rum
1 cup crushed ice

Combine the cream of coconut, fruit, rum, and half the crushed ice in a drink shaker, blender, or food processor. Serve in a chilled glass over the remaining crushed ice.

PUNCHES, SMOOTHIES, & SO FORTH

PLANTER'S PUNCH

SERVES 1

Picture yourself on a bougainvillea-framed verandah, fanning yourself and sipping this classic.

2 tsp. sugar
1 fl. oz. lemon or lime juice
1 fl. oz. orange juice
1½ fl. oz. light rum of your choice
1½ fl. oz. dark rum of your choice
dash of Grenadine (optional)
slice of pineapple, for garnishing

In a drink shaker, dissolve the sugar in the lemon or lime juice and orange juice. Add the rum, and Grenadine if using, fill the shaker with crushed ice and shake well. Stir it into a tall 10 fl. oz. glass with cracked ice. Garnish with the slice of pineapple, a cherry, a lemon or lime slice, ½ slice orange, or a sprig of mint. Serve with a straw.

TROPICAL FRUIT SMOOTHIES

SERVES 4

2 cups unsweetened orange juice
2 tbsp. powdered sugar
2 tbsp. fresh lime juice
2 cups sliced fresh strawberries, raspberries,
peaches, nectarines, banana, mango, papaya, guava
3 tbsp. complementary no-sugar-added fruit spread,
such as strawberry, peach, orange marmalade
1 tsp. vanilla extract
4 lime or orange slices or sprigs of mint (optional)

Combine the orange juice, sugar, and lime juice, and pour into an 8 inch square baking pan. Freeze until firm. Break the frozen juice mixture into chunks. Place the juice chunks, fruit, fruit spread, and vanilla extract in a blender or food processor, and process until smooth. Pour into glasses and serve immediately, garnished with lime or orange slices or a sprig of mint, if desired.

PIÑA FIZZ

SERVES 8

This can be served with or without liquor. Whip up a batch of each for your next party. Garnish the ones containing the rum with an orange slice, and you and your guests will be able to tell them apart.

1 cup orange juice
1 cup mango juice
1 pint pineapple juice
1 pint orange sherbet
1 tbsp. Grenadine
1 cup club soda
½ cup dry, light-bodied rum (optional)
½ tsp. Angostura bitters (optional)

Mix the juices, sherbet, and Grenadine in a blender or food processor until smooth. Stir in the club soda and rum and bitters if using, and serve in chilled glasses.

Papaya Citrus Shake

PAPAYA CITRUS SHAKE

SERVES 4

*1 papaya (about 1 lb.), peeled, seeded
and cut into $^{1}/_{2}$ inch pieces
$^{1}/_{2}$ cup fresh lime juice
1 pint lemon or lime sherbet
1 cup ice cubes
lime slices, to garnish*

Blend the papaya, lime juice, sherbet, and ice cubes in a blender or food processor until the mixture is smooth. Pour the mixture into chilled glasses and garnish with lime slices.

PEACHY MANGO SMOOTHIE

SERVES 4

*$2^{1}/_{2}$ cups orange-mango juice beverage
1 cup sliced ripe banana
$^{1}/_{2}$ cup peeled, sliced fresh peaches or nectarines
1 tbsp. sugar
1tsp. vanilla or almond extract*

Freeze the juice in an 8 inch square baking pan until firm. Break the frozen juice into chunks. Place the juice chunks and remaining ingredients in a blender or food processor, and process until smooth. Serve immediately.

Spanish-speaking islanders call frosty, fruit-and-milk concoctions batidos – or, literally, "beatens." Tropical fruit is often so lush and creamy that adding milk seems almost redundant – that is, until you taste these treats. You can use canned fruit, but drain it first and omit the sugar.

YOUR CHOICE BATIDO

SERVES 1

½ cup crushed ice
1 medium papaya, mango, banana, guava or mamey
sapote, peeled and cut into pieces (about 1 cup)
½ cup cold milk
½ cup vanilla ice cream, slightly softened
2 tbsp. sugar

Mix all the ingredients in a blender or food processor until smooth, and serve in a frosted glass.

PIÑA BATIDO

SERVES 2

1 pint milk
1 cup unsweetened pineapple juice, chilled
⅓ cup crushed ice
3 tbsp. sugar
2 tbsp. orange juice
1 tsp. lemon juice

Mix all the ingredients in a blender or food processor until smooth, and serve in frosted glasses.

PASSION FRUIT BATIDO

SERVES 2

1 pint milk
1 cup passion fruit nectar, chilled
⅓ cup crushed ice
sugar to taste
2 tbsp. orange juice
1 tsp. lemon juice

Mix all the ingredients in a blender or food processor until smooth, and serve in frosted glasses.

CHOCO-COCO-NANA MILKSHAKE

SERVES 4

1 pint low-fat milk
2 medium bananas, sliced
¼ cup chocolate-flavored syrup
1 tbsp. powdered sugar
¼ tsp. imitation coconut extract

Freeze the milk in an 8 inch square baking pan until firm. Leave to stand for 5 minutes and break into chunks. Place the milk chunks and remaining ingredients in a blender or food processor, and process until smooth. Serve immediately.

APPETIZERS, SANDWICHES, AND SNACKS

CONTENTS

DILLED SHRIMP IN
SMOKED KINGFISH BLANKET

SERVES 4–6

This is a sophisticated starter that might be served at any of the plush inns and resorts in the islands. Almost any thinly sliced smoked fish can be substituted for the Caribbean kingfish – just make certain skin and bones have been removed. Choose the plumpest shrimp, however, so that the treasure inside the "blanket" can be fully savored. A garnish of fresh dill and cherry tomatoes will add even more drama to the serving plate.

2 tbsp. fresh lime or lemon juice
½ tsp. salt
1 tbsp. chopped fresh cilantro
⅓ cup olive oil
1 tbsp. chopped fresh dill
white ground pepper
24 cooked shrimp, shelled and deveined
4 oz. smoked kingfish, thinly sliced and chilled

To garnish
fresh dill sprigs (optional)
cherry tomatoes (optional)

Combine the lime or lemon juice, salt, cilantro, olive oil, dill, and pepper in a glass bowl. Add the shrimp, cover, and marinate for 2 hours. Cut each slice of fish lengthwise into strips ¼ inch wide. Wind a fish strip around each shrimp and fasten with a cocktail toothpick. Garnish and serve.

SPICY MEAT PATTIES

SERVES 8–10 OR 16–20 IF MADE SMALLER

These popular Caribbean meat pastries are customized to suit personal taste by chefs everywhere – from Jamaica itself to Jamaica, New York. I use an untraditional cream cheese pastry for an elegant touch, but your old faithful pie crust dough will work just as well. If made bite-size small these make terrific appetizers. Leftovers may be frozen.

Pastry
1 cup all-purpose flour
¼ tsp. salt
½ cup chilled butter
½ cup soft cream cheese

Filling
1 tbsp. vegetable oil
1½ lb. lean beef, ground
1 medium onion, finely chopped
3 cloves garlic, minced
1 tbsp. hot pepper, seeded and minced
3 green onions, chopped
1 tbsp. curry powder
½ tsp. ground cumin
1 tbsp. ground thyme
⅓ cup finely ground cracker crumbs

½ cup beef or chicken bouillon
2 tbsp. finely chopped fresh cilantro
salt and fresh-ground black pepper

Sift the flour and salt together, and then blend in the butter and cream cheese with a pastry blender until the mixture looks like a bowl of small pebbles. Refrigerate for 24 hours.

Next day, preheat the oven to 450°F as you prepare the filling. In a medium skillet, heat the oil over medium heat. Add the beef, onion, garlic, hot pepper, and green onions. Fry, stirring constantly, until the beef is browned. Add the curry powder, cumin, thyme, cracker crumbs, bouillon, cilantro and salt and pepper to taste. Simmer, stirring frequently, for 20 minutes. Pour off any fat or liquid and set aside to cool.

While the filling cools, roll the dough to ⅛ inch thickness. Cut into rounds with a 3 inch diameter glass or cookie cutter. Put the rounds on a greased baking sheet. Place 1 tbsp. meat mixture in the middle of each round. Moisten the edges of each round, fold over and pinch together with a fork. Bake in the oven until golden brown, about 20 minutes.

CHICKEN CURRY ROTIS

SERVES 4–6

These are the island cousins of East Indian parathas or Mexican burritos. Called roti – which simply means bread – they're popular in Trinidad, Grenada, St. Lucia, and many other islands. You can serve the un-filled pooris as bread with any thick curried mixture or with the fillings for Spicy Meat Patties (page 31) or Stamp & Go Cod Cakes (page 34).

Pooris
4 cups wholewheat flour
2 tsp. salt
1 cup skim milk
2–3 tbsp. butter or ghee (page 17)
vegetable oil (for frying pooris
and for chicken mixture)

Chicken curry filling
1 lb. chicken, skinned, boned,
and cut into 1 1/2 inch cubes
1 medium onion, finely chopped
1/2 tsp. minced garlic
1/4 tsp. hot pepper sauce
1/2 tsp. salt
1 tbsp. curry powder
1/8 tsp. ground ginger
1/8 tsp. ground cumin
1/4 tbsp. fresh-ground black pepper
1/4 cup dry white wine
2 cooking apples, cored, chopped, cooked until soft
and drained (optional)

To make the pooris, sift the flour and salt together into a small bowl. Slowly dribble the skim milk into the flour and salt mixture. (If the dough is too dry, add a little more milk, a tiny drop at a time.) Knead for about 5 minutes until the dough is smooth. Refrigerate, in a tightly covered container, overnight.

Next day, divide the dough in half and roll each half to a thickness of 1/4 inch. Cut each rolled circle into smaller circles 6–8 inches in diameter. (I cut with the rim of a cereal bowl.) The dough will be pliable so you can stretch it by pressing down on each circle with the palm of your hand. You should have about 8 circles in all. If you have any dough left, roll it into an extra poori or two. Spread each circle of dough with butter or ghee and fold in half. Using your fingers, spread the butter or ghee generously on top of the halved circle, covering the entire surface, and fold again two more times, each time spreading butter or ghee on both sides of the dough wedge. Set aside, covered.

Combine the chicken, onion, garlic, hot pepper sauce, salt, curry powder, ginger, cumin, pepper, and wine in a bowl, and marinate for 2 hours, turning occasionally. Drain away the liquid. Then place the oil in a saucepan and heat to medium. Add the chicken and cook, stirring constantly, for about 5 minutes, then lower the heat and simmer for about 5 minutes or until the chicken is tender. Add the apples, if using, and keep warm.

Unfold the circles of dough. Add the oil to a heavy-based skillet to a level of 1/4 inch and heat until a drop of water sputters in it. Place two pooris at a time in the skillet and fry each side for about 2 minutes or until lightly browned. Wrap in a clean tea towel or place on a warming tray to keep warm. The oil must be sizzling hot so, after doing each batch of pooris, add a little more oil and allow it to heat up until a drop of water sputters in it again.

When the last poori is cooked, place 2 tbsp. chicken mixture into each one, fold in half twice and serve. If the finished rotis are cold, fry in a small amount of oil until heated or reheat in a microwave oven, wrapping each in a couple of layers of slightly damp paper towels. Reheat the pooris according to the manufacturer's directions for reheating pastries.

ISLAND SHRIMP PITA CANAPÉS

SERVES 4–6

In this recipe the shrimp are marinated in a spicy vinaigrette, which gives them their punch. They can be marinated overnight, which makes this a perfect make-ahead dish for a party. All you need to do on the day is toast the pita!

¼ cup cider vinegar
⅓ cup vegetable oil
½ tbsp. sugar
1 tsp. Worcestershire sauce
¼ tsp. hot pepper sauce (page 96)
½ tsp. English-style dry mustard
1 tsp. peeled and minced fresh ginger root
salt and fresh-ground black pepper
8 oz. medium shrimp, shelled and deveined
⅛ cup thinly sliced red bell pepper
⅛ cup thinly sliced yellow bell pepper
⅛ cup thinly sliced green bell pepper
⅛ cup cilantro, finely chopped

dried hot red pepper flakes (optional)
4 large, or 8 small, pita pockets, cut into about
12 wedges and toasted lightly
cilantro sprigs, to garnish

In a saucepan, whisk together the vinegar, oil, sugar, Worcestershire sauce, hot pepper sauce, mustard, ginger root, and salt and pepper to taste. Bring the mixture to a boil and simmer it, stirring occasionally, for 5 minutes. Add the shrimp and simmer, stirring occasionally, for 3 to 5 minutes, or until they are cooked through. Transfer the mixture to a heatproof bowl and add the peppers, tossing the mixture well. Chill, covered, for at least 2 hours, or overnight.

Drain the mixture, discarding the liquid, and stir in the cilantro, red pepper flakes if using, and salt and pepper to taste. Arrange the shrimp and several pepper strips on each pita wedge, and garnish with cilantro sprigs.

STAMP AND GO COD CAKES

Once sold from humble seaside shacks in Jamaica, these codfish cakes were wrapped in paper and stamped "paid" – hence the name Stamp and Go. People on the Spanish-speaking islands call salted cod *bacalao* and eat very similar cod fritters. Cod was salted out of necessity in the days before refrigeration and the custom continues today.

8 oz. salt codfish fillets
1 cup all-purpose flour
1 tsp. baking powder
1/4 tsp. salt
1 egg, lightly beaten
3/4 cup milk
1 tbsp. unsalted butter, melted
2 medium onions, chopped
1/2 tsp. chopped hot pepper or 1/4 tsp. chili powder
vegetable oil for frying

Rinse the codfish under cold, running water for 2–3 minutes, and place in a bowl of water to soak overnight. Drain, rinse and place in a saucepan with boiling water to cover. Simmer gently, covered, for about 20 minutes. Drain, remove the bones and skin, and shred the fish finely with your fingers, inspecting carefully for small bones.

Sift the flour, baking powder, and salt together. Combine the egg, milk, and butter, and stir into the dry ingredients. Add the cod, onion, and pepper, and mix well. Heat the oil in a heavy-based saucepan until it reaches a temperature of 375° and drop in the fish mixture a teaspoonful at a time. Deep fry until golden brown. Drain on paper towels and serve hot.

CONCH SCOTCH BONNET FRITTERS WITH TWO COOL DIPS

SERVES 4–6

1 lb, conch, clams or squid
3 celery stalks, finely chopped
1 onion, finely chopped
1/2 cup butter
1 tsp. minced hot pepper
pinch of thyme
pinch of basil
pinch of oregano
pinch of salt
pinch of fresh-ground black pepper
1/4 tsp. baking powder
4 eggs
1 1/2 cups all-purpose flour
splash of milk
vegetable oil for deep frying

Lime Dip
1 1/4 cups sour cream
1/3 cup mayonnaise
juice of 2 limes

Avocado-Cress Dip
1 small ripe avocado, peeled and pitted

1/2 tbsp. milk
1/2 tbsp. lemon juice
3/4 tsp. salt
1/4 cup loosely packed watercress, tough stems removed

Put the seafood through a meat grinder or food processor. Fry the celery and onion in the butter for about 3 minutes. Add the hot pepper, herbs, salt, and pepper, and stir to blend thoroughly. Place the mixture in a large bowl together with the seafood, baking powder, eggs, flour, and milk. Mix well to a thick yet runny consistency and chill.

While the fritter batter is chilling, prepare the dips by mixing the ingredients in a food processor with the knife blade attached or a blender at medium speed. Place the dips in the refrigerator to chill, about 30 minutes.

When the fritter batter is chilled, heat the oil to 350° for frying. Using a large oval spoon, form 1 inch thick dumplings and drop them straight into the hot oil. Cook for about 4–6 minutes. Drain on paper towels and serve with the dips.

CREAM CHEESE CURRIED CANAPÉS

SERVES 4–6

Here's an easy-to-make tea sandwich that is a creative garnisher's dream. You can top these canapés with all sorts of goodies, such as minced chives, chopped walnuts, slivered toasted almonds, sliced green onion, watercress, raisins, toasted flaked coconut, a dollop of chutney, a chunk of fresh mango, or papaya – you name it.

4 × 8 oz. packages cream cheese, softened
⅛ cup orange marmalade
1 tsp. curry powder
8 thin slices white bread

Beat the cream cheese with an electric mixer set at medium speed until it is fluffy. Stir in the marmalade and curry powder. Cut 2 × 2 inch rounds out of each bread slice with a cookie cutter. Spread 1½ tsp. cream cheese mixture on each bread round. Garnish as desired.

CRUNCHY FRIED SHRIMP CANAPÉS WITH GINGERY MAYO

SERVES 4–6

An array of textures and colors and the ginger-scented shrimp make this appetizer one for special occasions. These are nice to pass round with cocktails, or with aperitifs before a dinner party because they are not too filling.

1½ lb. cooked small shrimp, shelled and deveined
all-purpose flour seasoned with salt and cayenne pepper
vegetable oil for deep-frying
2 tbsp. peeled and minced ginger root
⅔ cup mayonnaise
3 tbsp. Dijon-style mustard
4 slices rye bread, cut into 2 inch rounds
and toasted lightly
10 radishes, trimmed and thinly sliced
1 cup alfalfa sprouts
watercress or cilantro, to garnish (optional)
2 tsp. fresh lemon juice

Toss the shrimp with seasoned flour in a bag to coat them. Transfer them to a sieve and shake off excess flour. Heat 1 inch oil over moderately high heat until it registers 375° on a deep-fat thermometer and fry the shrimp in batches, stirring occasionally, for 1 minute, or until they are just cooked through. Transfer them to paper towels to drain.

In a small bowl, stir together the ginger root, mayonnaise, and mustard until the mixture is combined well and spread 1 tbsp. of this ginger-mayonnaise mixture on each piece of toast. Arrange the radishes, alfalfa sprouts, and shrimp on top of each canapé. Place on a serving platter and garnish with watercress or cilantro. Stir lemon juice into the remaining mayonnaise and serve canapés with the mayonnaise drizzled over them.

SMOKY FISH PÂTÉ

SERVES 6—8

You may use any smoked fish for this tangy pâté. Serve with an assortment of crackers.

1 lb. smoked marlin
¹⁄₂ cup sweet pickle relish
¹⁄₄ cup prepared horseradish sauce
1 small onion, chopped
1 celery stalk, peeled and finely chopped
¹⁄₂ tsp. lime juice
1 tsp. hot pepper sauce (page 96)
¹⁄₃ cup mayonnaise
salt and fresh-ground black pepper

Coarsely chop the fish and place in a mixing bowl. Add the relish, horseradish, onion, celery, and lime juice, and mix well. Add half the hot pepper sauce and half the mayonnaise. Blend together and taste. Add more hot sauce, according to your taste. Add more mayonnaise and mix until desired texture and taste is achieved.

SALADS

CONTENTS

CREOLE SPINACH SALAD

SERVES 4

This zippy salad complements any main dish, even standards such as roast beef. Top with wedges of red ripe tomatoes and paper-thin slices of cucumber.

1 lb. fresh spinach, cleaned and stemmed
1 red onion, thinly sliced
jerk croutons (page 92)
2 tbsp. roasted pecan nuts, finely chopped
¼ cup plain yogurt
¼ cup prepared mustard, any type
2 tbsp. lime or lemon juice
2 tbsp. balsamic vinegar
1 tsp. dry jerk seasoning of your choice (page 92)
hot pepper sauce (page 96) to taste

ground white pepper to taste
¼ cup chicken stock

To garnish
tomato wedges
cucumber slices

In a large bowl, toss together the spinach, red onion, jerk croutons, and pecan nuts. Blend the yogurt, mustard, lime or lemon juice, vinegar, jerk seasoning, hot pepper sauce, and white pepper in a blender or food processor until smooth, about 1 minute. With the motor running, slowly pour in the stock. Pour the dressing over the salad and croutons, and toss well.

SHRIMP AND LOBSTER SALAD TROPICAL
SERVES 4

Serve this lush delight with a crescent of sliced mango on your serving platter as they do at some of the most luxurious island inns. Pair with a vivid, frosty fruit daiquiri, and you will almost feel the lilting breezes and hear the steel drums.

1 lb. cooked shrimp, shelled and deveined
2 × 5 oz. cans lobster, drained and broken into
½ inch pieces
1 fresh mango, cubed
1 green bell pepper, thinly sliced
½ onion, thinly sliced
1 cup thinly sliced celery
2 cups cubed pineapple
½ cup plain yogurt
½ cup sour cream

½ cup fresh orange juice
4 tsp. fresh lime juice
2 tsp. grated ginger root

To garnish
lettuce leaves (optional)
crescent slices of mango

Combine the shrimp, lobster, mango, green pepper, onion, celery, and pineapple in a bowl and chill, covered, in the refrigerator. In a small bowl, whisk together the yogurt, sour cream, orange juice, lime juice, and ginger. In a serving bowl, gently toss the chilled shrimp, fruits, and vegetables. Pour the dressing over the salad and serve over lettuce leaves, if desired, and garnish with a crescent of mango slices.

CURRIED WILD RICE AND
JERKED CHICKEN SALAD

The main components of this snappy dish can be prepared ahead and combined at the last minute with the raisins, green onion, and nuts.

4 jerked chicken breasts (prepared according to any recipe in Jerked Dishes section), chilled and cut into bite-sized pieces
1 bunch of green onions, chopped (including the green part)
1 cup golden raisins
½ cup slivered almonds
lettuce leaves, to garnish (optional)

Dressing
2 cloves garlic, chopped
3 tbsp. white wine vinegar
4 tbsp. fresh lime juice
1½ tbsp. curry powder
3 tbsp. mango chutney
salt and fresh-ground black pepper
⅔ cup olive oil
¾ cup sour cream
3 tbsp. water
½ cup finely chopped cilantro

Rice Mixture
4–6 cups cooked wild rice, prepared according to package directions
1 tbsp. white wine vinegar
2 tbsp. olive oil
salt and fresh-ground black pepper

Make the dressing first. In a blender or food processor, combine the garlic, vinegar, lime juice, curry powder, chutney, and salt and pepper to taste until the mixture is smooth. With the motor running, add the oil in a stream, then the sour cream and water, adding additional water if necessary to reach the desired consistency. Transfer the dressing to a small bowl and stir in the cilantro. Cover and chill in the refrigerator.

To make the rice mixture, place the cooked rice in a bowl, add the vinegar, oil, and salt and pepper, and toss vigorously. Cover and chill in the refrigerator.

Just before serving, toss together the wild rice mixture, the chicken, and the dressing. Mix in the green onion, raisins, and almonds and serve on lettuce leaves if desired.

CURRIED TUNA SALAD
WITH TROPICAL FRUIT

SERVES 4–6

2 × 6½ oz. cans white tuna in water,
drained and flaked
1½ cups mango or papaya, diced and drained well
1½ cups chopped celery
½ cup papaya seeds, ground to size of peppercorns
(optional)
½ cup shredded carrots
¼ cup chopped green onions
¼ cup chopped red onion
¾ cup mayonnaise

½ tsp. curry powder
lettuce leaves

Combine the tuna, mango or papaya, celery, papaya seeds if using, half the carrots and green, and red onion in a bowl. Combine the mayonnaise and curry powder in a small bowl, then add to the tuna mixture and toss gently to mix. Cover and chill. Spoon the salad into a lettuce-lined serving dish. Sprinkle the remaining carrot over the salad for garnish.

JICAMA OR WATER CHESTNUT, ORANGE, AND
BROILED ONION SALAD WITH RUM FRENCH DRESSING

SERVES 4

This dish is a symphony of flavors and textures with sweet onion as the star.

1 medium jicama (1 lb.), or water chestnuts,
peeled and sliced into ½ inch pieces
2 oranges, peeled and separated into sections
with pith removed
8 oz. sweet onion
4 tbsp. olive oil
1 tbsp. lime juice
1 tbsp. light rum
1 tsp. minced green onion
1 tsp. minced parsley
¼ tsp. dry mustard
dash of Worcestershire sauce
salt and fresh-ground black pepper
toasted jerk croutons (page 92) (optional)

Combine the jicama and orange in a serving bowl, and set aside. Preheat the broiler. Slice the onion crosswise ¼ inch thick, keeping the slices intact. Brush lightly with about 1½ tbsp. olive oil and arrange in a basket or broiler pan. Sprinkle salt over them and broil for 5–8 minutes until they begin to char slightly. Turn and broil for 5 minutes longer, until soft and charred just on top. Separate into rings and add to the jicama and orange mixture.

Whisk the remaining olive oil with the lime juice, rum, green onion, parsley, mustard, Worcestershire sauce, and salt and pepper. Pour over the salad, and serve.

BLACK-EYED PEA AND PASTA SALAD
WITH ZESTY DRESSING

SERVES 4

This tastes great with any jerked dish and can be made up to a day ahead.

Dressing
1/4 cup olive oil
2 tbsp. tarragon, malt or balsamic vinegar
1 tbsp. Dijon-style mustard
3/4 tsp. minced garlic
1/4 tsp. ground cumin
1/2 tsp. sugar
1/2 tsp. salt
1/2 tsp. finely grated orange rind
dash of hot pepper sauce (page 96)

8 oz. macaroni, pasta twists or tortellini,
cooked al dente and rinsed immediately under cold
running water

15 oz. can black-eyed peas,
rinsed and drained
1 medium tomato, seeded and diced
2/3 cup ripe black or green olives, sliced (optional)
2/3 cup chopped red bell pepper
2/3 cup chopped green bell pepper
5 oz. jicama or water chestnuts, diced
1/2 cup sliced green onions
1/4 cup chopped fresh cilantro

In a blender, food processor or bowl, combine the oil, vinegar, mustard, garlic, cumin, sugar, salt, orange rind, and hot pepper sauce. Blend until smooth.

Place the pasta, black-eyed peas, tomato, olives, peppers, jicama or water chestnuts, onion, and cilantro in a large serving bowl. Add the dressing and toss gently to mix and coat. Cover and chill.

CRAB-STUFFED TOMATOES

SERVES 2

Try to use a homemade hot pepper sauce (see Jerked Dishes) with this or a very good prepared hot sauce from the islands. A touch of hot, hot, hot is what gives the dish its special island flair.

2 cups lump crab meat, thawed and drained if frozen
²/₃ cup seeded and chopped ripe tomatoes
²/₃ cup diced seedless cucumber
2 hard-cooked eggs, chopped
²/₃ cup mayonnaise
¹/₄ cup hot pepper sauce (page 96)
2 tbsp. sour cream
2 tsp. lime juice
1 tbsp. minced chives
salt and fresh-ground black pepper
2 large ripe tomatoes
1 soft-leafed lettuce, rinsed and dried

In a bowl, blend together the crab, chopped tomatoes, cucumber, and eggs, and chill. Blend the mayonnaise, hot pepper sauce, sour cream, lime juice, chives, and salt and pepper, and chill.

Without cutting all the way through the bottoms, core the whole tomatoes and cut them into sixths, forming tulip shapes. Line 2 plates with the lettuce, center the tomatoes on the lettuce, and mound the crab salad on top. Serve the salad with remaining sauce.

SPICY BLACK BEAN AND HAM HOCK SALAD

SERVES 4

This tastes best made from scratch, but if you're in a hurry, here's a no-cook version: simply substitute 2 × 1 lb. cans beans, drained and rinsed, and stir in ground versions of the spices and any minced cooked ham or pork. Whip up the vinaigrette in the same manner as below.

8 oz. black beans
2 large ham hocks
1 large bay leaf
1 tsp. coriander seeds, cracked
1 tsp. cumin seeds, crushed
1 tsp. red chili pepper flakes
¼ tsp. ground cinnamon
¼ cup lime juice
1 tbsp. sherry vinegar
1 tsp. ground cumin
1 tbsp. olive oil
1 tbsp. hot pepper sauce (page 96)
1 clove garlic, crushed
2 tbsp. finely chopped bell red pepper
2 tbsp. finely chopped green onion
salt and fresh-ground black pepper
½ cup whole cilantro leaves, stems removed, rinsed and dried

Soak the beans, if necessary, according to the directions on the package. Place the beans in a Dutch oven. Add the ham hocks, bay leaf, coriander seeds, cumin seeds, chili flakes, and cinnamon. Add fresh cold water to cover. Simmer gently over medium heat until the beans are tender, about 45 minutes. Remove the ham hocks and set aside to cool. Remove the bay leaf and discard. Drain the beans and rinse under cold running water until chilled. Set aside.

Combine the lime juice and sherry vinegar in a non-reactive bowl. Whisk in the ground cumin, olive oil, hot pepper sauce, and garlic. Stir in the red pepper, green onion, and salt and pepper to taste. Set aside.

Pull the ham off the hock, discarding the bone and fat. Grind the meat and place it in a salad bowl. Add the beans and cilantro. Pour the vinaigrette over the mixture and toss to combine. Season to taste with salt, pepper, and additional hot sauce.

MANGO-STARFRUIT SALAD WITH GINGER VINAIGRETTE

SERVES 4

This vinaigrette tastes great sprinkled over boniato chips, fried green plantains, green salads, and even jerk dishes.

4 cubed mangoes
4 starfruits, sliced crosswise for star shapes
¼ cup grated ginger root
½ cup olive oil
½ cup cider vinegar
2 tbsp. fresh lime juice
1 tsp. Dijon-style mustard
1 tsp. minced cilantro
¼ tsp. minced green onion
¼ tsp. salt
¼ tsp fresh-ground black pepper

Combine the mangoes and starfruit, and chill. Purée the ginger, olive oil, vinegar, lime juice, mustard, cilantro, green onion, salt, and pepper until smooth in a food processor or blender, or by hand. Drizzle over the chilled fruit.

WATERCRESS SALAD WITH ZINGY PEPPER DRESSING

SERVES 4

This is not for those who like tame, bland salads. This one has the bitiness of watercress, the sweetness of fresh tomato, and a delectable mustardy hot pepper heat. It will enliven any plain main dish.

2 bunches watercress, washed, trimmed and dried
1 large ripe tomato, cut into bite-sized pieces
1 small onion, thinly sliced, rings separated
1 tbsp. red wine vinegar
1 tbsp. chicken stock
1 tbsp. hot pepper sauce (page 96)
½ tsp. minced garlic
¼ tsp. Dijon-style mustard
salt and fresh-ground black pepper

In a large bowl, combine the watercress, tomato, and onion. In a small bowl, whisk together the vinegar, chicken stock, hot pepper sauce, garlic, and mustard. Season with salt and pepper. Drizzle over the salad and toss gently to coat.

Mango-Starfruit Salad with Ginger Vinaigrette

PAPAYA-CITRUS SALAD WITH
PAPAYA SEED DRESSING

SERVES 4

This cool and refreshing salad is a nice foil for a spicy jerked dish. The dressing is quite versatile – make an extra batch and use on coleslaw, fruit, or green salad.

1 small red onion, halved and thinly sliced
1 orange, sectioned, with 2 tbsp. juice reserved
2 grapefruits, preferably pink, sectioned
½ ripe papaya (about 8 oz.), coarsely sliced
1 red bell pepper, cored, seeded
and thinly sliced
1 yellow bell pepper, cored, seeded
and thinly sliced

Dressing
⅓ cup sugar
1½ tsp. salt
¼ tsp. Dijon-style mustard
3 tbsp. white vinegar
½ cup vegetable oil
2 tbsp. papaya seeds

Place the onion in a small bowl. Cover with ice water and leave to stand for 30 minutes at room temperature. Drain and dry on paper towels.

Combine the orange and grapefruit sections with the onion, papaya, red pepper, and yellow pepper in a large salad bowl.

In a blender or food processor, blend together the sugar, salt, mustard, and vinegar until blended well. With the motor running, add the oil in a stream and blend until smooth. Add the seeds and blend until they are about the size of peppercorns. Drizzle the dressing over the salad and toss well.

ISLAND FRUIT SALAD

SERVES 4

Add cooked shrimp to the marinade and this becomes a regal salad.

11 tbsp. balsamic vinegar
juice from 1 orange
2 tsp. soy sauce
2 tbsp. vegetable oil
¹/₄ tsp. salt
¹/₂ tsp. sugar (optional)
2 medium oranges, peeled and sectioned,
reserving juice
1 cup canned unsweetened grapefruit sections,
drained

1 starfruit, kiwi or pear, sliced
1 lb. cooked medium shrimp, shelled and deveined
1 medium red onion, thinly sliced
lettuce leaves or two avocados, to garnish (optional)

In a blender or food processor or by hand, blend the vinegar, orange juice, soy sauce, oil, salt, and sugar until smooth. Transfer to a bowl and add the orange and grapefruit sections, starfruit, kiwi or pear slices, shrimp and onion. Marinate, covered, in the refrigerator for 1 hour. Drain the fruit and onion of liquid and serve on lettuce-lined plates or in halved, pitted avocados, partially scooped out.

BLACK BEANS AND RICE SALAD

SERVES 4–6

If you have some leftover cooked rice on hand, this dish can be whipped up in just a few minutes at the can opener and chopping board. It makes a filling, nutritious accompaniment to any light main dish. For color, lay strips of pimiento or red bell pepper across the top of the dish.

*2 cups cooked or canned black beans,
rinsed and drained
2 cups cooked rice
1¹/₂ cups fresh cilantro
¹/₄ cup lime juice
³/₄ cup oil*

*¹/₂ cup chopped onion
2 cloves garlic, crushed
salt and fresh-ground black pepper
pimiento or red bell pepper strips, to garnish
(optional)*

Mix the beans, rice, and cilantro together in a bowl. Place the lime juice in a small bowl and whisk in the oil. Add the onion and garlic, and toss with the beans. Add salt and pepper to taste, and garnish with pimiento or red bell pepper. Serve at room temperature or chilled.

TROPICAL PORK SALAD WITH ORANGE-MINT DRESSING

SERVES 4

Here's a marvellous way to use up leftover pork. (You might just find yourself cooking pork so you can make this delicious salad!)

1 tsp. finely grated orange rind
¼ cup fresh orange juice
1½ tbsp. cider vinegar
2 tbsp. chopped fresh mint leaves or 1 tbsp. dried
¾ tsp. Dijon-style mustard
¼ tsp. salt
¼ tsp. fresh-ground pepper
½ cup olive oil
2 cups shredded cooked pork
1 large ripe papaya (1 lb.) peeled, halved, seeded and cut into ½ inch chunks

1 ripe avocado (10 oz.) halved, pitted, peeled and cut into ½ inch chunks
1 small red onion, thinly sliced (½ cup)
6 cups lettuce, fresh spinach or chicory torn into pieces
⅓ cup sliced almonds, toasted

Whisk together the orange rind and juice, vinegar, mint, mustard, salt, and pepper in a large bowl. Gradually whisk in the oil until blended. Gently stir in the pork, papaya, avocado, and onion, tossing to mix and coat. Mound the salad on a serving platter lined with lettuce, spinach or chicory and sprinkle with almonds.

S O U P S

CALLALOO
SERVES 4–6

No matter what its spelling – calaloo, callilu, callau, kalalou, or callaloo – this soup is celebrated throughout the multi-ethnic Caribbean. Its name is taken from its chief ingredient, the leaves of the tuberous taro or callaloo plant, but cooks outside the Caribbean have found that fresh spinach, Swiss chard, kale, and Indian bhaji are quite similar to callaloo and a lot easier to track down. Mint-green in color and with a subtle, sharp flavor, the soup makes a refreshing opener for any meal. West Indians would protest about omitting okra, but if you don't like its astringent taste rest assured that callaloo's distinctive flavor does not suffer for lack of it. If you are entertaining, try stirring in some lump crab meat.

8 oz. fresh spinach, Swiss chard or Indian bhaji
4 oz. okra, sliced (optional)
8 oz. eggplant, peeled and chopped
into bite-sized pieces
4 cups water
1 tbsp. vegetable oil
2 onions, finely chopped
2 cloves garlic, minced
1/2 tsp. thyme
1/4 tsp. allspice
2 tbsp. chopped chives
1 fresh hot pepper, seeded and chopped,
or 1 tbsp. hot pepper sauce (page 96)
1 tbsp. white wine vinegar
1 cup coconut milk (page 14)
salt and fresh-ground black pepper

Wash and drain the greens, discarding the stems. Chop the leaves into pieces. Place in a large, heavy-based saucepan with the okra, if using, and the eggplant. Add the water and cook over medium heat until the vegetables are tender, about 15 minutes. (If you have added okra, check frequently as this vegetable tends to become glutinous if overcooked.) Heat the oil in a heavy skillet and sauté the onions and garlic until the onions are translucent. Add the remaining ingredients, plus the onions and garlic, to vegetables, and simmer for about 5 minutes. Purée in a blender or food processor and serve immediately.

BAHAMIAN CONCH CHOWDER
SERVES 4–6

Conch chowder is to the Caribbean what chicken soup is to most of the rest of the world – it's ubiquitous and good. Conch is the shoe-leather tough meat of those beautiful big shells you can hear the ocean in.

1 slice bacon, chopped
½ tbsp. vegetable oil
½ cup chopped carrots
1 cup chopped celery
1 cup chopped onion
¼ cup chopped green bell pepper
¼ cup chopped red bell pepper
1 tbsp. minced garlic
1 lb. conch, ground
8 oz. can crushed tomatoes
1 tbsp. tomato paste
1 bay leaf
1 tsp. dried thyme
½ tsp. black pepper
1½–2 quarts fish stock or chicken broth
1 large potato, peeled and diced (about 3½ cups)
¼ cup cream sherry
salt
cayenne pepper
vegetable oil (optional)
all-purpose flour (optional)

In a 3–4 quart Dutch oven or saucepan set over medium heat, cook the bacon in the oil for 2 minutes. Add the carrots, celery, onion, green and red pepper, and garlic. Sauté until the onion is translucent. Add the conch, crushed tomatoes, tomato paste, bay leaf, thyme, pepper, and fish or chicken stock (using the lower measurement for a heartier chowder). Bring to a boil, reduce the heat and simmer, uncovered, for 30–45 minutes, or until the stock is reduced by about a third.

Add the potatoes and cook, uncovered, for about 20 minutes or until the potatoes are very tender and the chowder is thickened. Stir in the sherry, salt, and cayenne pepper to taste.

To thicken the chowder, add a roux of vegetable oil and flour – about ½ tbsp. oil to 1½ tbsp. flour. Stir it in until the chowder reaches the desired thickness.

CALABAZA SOUP
SERVES 4–6

You may substitute Hubbard or butternut squash or even zucchini for the calabaza in this smooth, rich, nutty-tasting dish. If using small squashes or zucchini, simply parboil until tender. Calabaza is huge, and is usually sold in quarters or halves.

3 lb. calabaza
4 tbsp. butter
¼ cup pine nuts, ground into paste
2 large onions, chopped
2 tsp. ground coriander
1 tsp. ground cumin
½ tsp. ground white pepper
1 tsp. salt
3 cups chicken stock
1 ripe plantain, peeled and cut into ¼ inch slices
1 cup mango or apple juice, peach nectar or cider

Preheat the oven to 350°. Cut the calabaza in half if it is whole, then remove and discard seeds. Place the calabaza flesh-side down on a cookie sheet and bake for approximately 30 minutes.

While the calabaza is baking, melt the butter over medium heat in a large soup pot, gradually adding the pine nut paste. Add the onions, coriander, cumin, pepper, and salt. Cover and cook until the onions are soft, about 20 minutes.

Add the chicken stock to the pot and bring to a boil over high heat. When the soup is boiling, add the sliced plantain. Cover the pot and reduce the heat to medium. Simmer for 10 minutes.

Remove the calabaza from the oven and allow to cool enough to handle. Scoop out the calabaza flesh, break it into small pieces and add it to the soup. Add the fruit juice and simmer for 30 minutes until the plantain is tender.

Pour the soup through a strainer, reserving the liquid in a large pot. Transfer the solid ingredients from the strainer to a blender or food processor. Process until smooth.

Return the purée and liquid to the pot. Cover and simmer over low heat until hot. If you wish to thicken the soup, uncover and cook over low heat, stirring frequently, until it thickens. Serve hot.

ICED PASSION FRUIT SOUP WITH YOGURT AND VANILLA
SERVES 4

Look for passion fruits that are large and heavy with dimpled skin. They are quite expensive so you'll probably want to reserve this recipe for a special occasion.

20 fresh passion fruits
1/2 cup sugar
4 inch piece of vanilla bean, split lengthwise
1 cup water
2 tsp. unflavored gelatin
1/2 cup plain yogurt, whisked well
fresh mint leaves, to garnish (optional)

Place a coarse sieve over a medium non-reactive saucepan. Working over the sieve, cut each passion fruit in half, and scoop out the pulp with a teaspoon. Push the pulp and juice through the sieve, and discard the seeds.

Add the sugar, vanilla bean and water to the saucepan and bring to a simmer over low heat, stirring. Remove from the heat and sprinkle the gelatin evenly over the mixture. Set aside, undisturbed, to let the gelatin thicken on the surface of the juice, about 3 minutes. Then whisk the mixture well to incorporate the gelatin. Set a fine sieve over a medium non-reactive bowl and strain the mixture. Leave to cool to room temperature, then place the bowl in a larger bowl filled with ice and water. Chill the mixture over the ice, stirring frequently. (The recipe can be prepared to this point and refrigerated overnight.)

To serve, ladle the chilled soup into 4 shallow soup dishes. Top each serving with 2 tbsp. yogurt and top with mint leaves if desired.

ISLAND POTATO VICHYSSOISE
SERVES 6–8

This refreshing soup can be made with breadfruit or you can substitute sweet potatoes. It is quite elegant, especially when served in chilled bowls and garnished with chives or cilantro.

1 3/4 cups sliced green onions, including a small amount of the tops
5 cups chicken stock or broth
2 1/2 lb. breadfruit, peeled, cored, diced, boiled in salted water until tender (about 25 minutes) and strained or sweet potatoes, baked in their skins until soft
salt and white pepper
1/2 cup light cream or half-and-half
fresh chives or cilantro, chopped, to garnish (optional)

Combine the onions with 1 cup stock, and simmer until tender, about 15 minutes. If using sweet potatoes, scoop out the cooked pulp, discard the skins, and measure out about 3 cups pulp. Purée the breadfruit or sweet potato pulp with the onion-stock mixture until smooth. Simmer for a few minutes with the remaining stock. Add salt and pepper to taste. Cool and refrigerate until ready to use. Garnish with chives or cilantro if desired.

PINEAPPLE-MANGO BISQUE
SERVES 4

3 tbsp. sugar
2 tbsp. dark rum
2 tbsp. water
3 lb. pineapple, peeled, cored and cut into 1 in. pieces
2 mangoes, peeled, pitted and cut into ¹/₂ inch pieces
3 cups cold milk
pinch of cinnamon
¹/₂ cup chilled heavy cream, plus more for serving

In a small saucepan, combine the sugar, rum, and water. Bring to a boil over high heat and boil until reduced slightly, 1–2 minutes. Remove from the heat and set aside to cool.

In a blender or food processor, combine the pineapple, mangoes, and rum syrup with ¹/₂ cup milk, and purée until smooth. Strain the soup through a coarse strainer set over a large non-reactive bowl. Whisk in the remaining milk, the cinnamon, and the cream. Cover and refrigerate until well chilled, 4–24 hours.

TOMATO-ORANGE SOUP

SERVES 4

The orange in this soup brings out the sweet-acidic flavor of homegrown beefsteak tomatoes, if you are lucky enough to have some. Serve with jerk croutons for an extra treat for the taste buds.

2¼ lb. ripe tomatoes, blanched, peeled and
quartered (or canned whole tomatoes, undrained)
½ cup firmly packed fresh basil leaves
3 × ½ inch strip orange peel
2 tbsp. chopped green onion (white part only)
1 tsp. sugar
2 tbsp. lime or lemon juice
1 cup orange juice
1 tbsp. cornstarch
2 tbsp. minced cilantro, chives or parsley
salt and fresh-ground black pepper
jerk croutons (page 92)

Combine the tomatoes, basil, orange peel, green onion, sugar, and lime or lemon juice in a medium saucepan. Cover and bring to a boil. Lower the heat immediately and simmer, covered, for 15 minutes. Remove the orange peel. Purée the mixture in a blender or food processor and strain through a sieve if desired to discard any seeds.

Return the liquid to the saucepan. Stir together the orange juice and cornstarch in a small bowl until smooth. Stir into the tomato mixture. Cook over medium heat, stirring constantly, until the mixture thickens and comes to a boil. Lower the heat, stir in the cilantro, chives or parsley, and salt and pepper to taste. Garnish with jerk croutons, if desired.

COCONUT SHRIMP SOUP

SERVES 4

1 red bell pepper, diced
1½ tbsp. chopped green onions,
including a small amount of green tops
2 cups homemade chicken stock or canned,
with fat strained out
2 tsp. chopped garlic
1 tbsp. grated ginger root
1 tbsp. ground coriander
½ tbsp. curry powder
½ tsp. thyme
½ tsp. white pepper
½ tsp. hot pepper sauce (page 96)
1¾ cups coconut milk (page 14)
1¼ lb. medium shrimp, shelled and deveined
1 cup heavy cream

In a small bowl, mix together the red pepper and green onion, and set aside.

In a 4 quart Dutch oven or saucepan over medium-high heat, bring the chicken stock, garlic, ginger, coriander, curry powder, thyme, pepper, hot pepper sauce, and coconut milk to a boil. Reduce the heat immediately and simmer for about 5 minutes. Remove from the heat and skim any fat off the top. Return to medium-high heat, bring to a simmer and add half the pepper and green onion mixture, and the shrimp. Simmer just until the shrimp is done, about 5 minutes. Do not overcook. Remove from the heat and stir in the cream. Taste and adjust the seasoning. Ladle into bowls and garnish with the remaining red pepper and green onion mixture.

SPICY CHICKEN SOUP

SERVES 4

This island-style soup is anything but bland – it has a well-seasoned, true chicken flavor and the vegetables added toward the end have freshness, color and lots of nutrients. Pair with a sandwich for lunch or start a meal off with it – or try adding some of the chicken, shredded or diced, and some noodles for a meal-in-a-dish.

1 onion, halved
2 celery stalks, including leaves, diced
2 carrots, diced
1 parsnip, diced
5 cloves garlic, peeled
3 lb. stewing chicken
1½ quarts water
½ tsp. minced fresh basil
½ tsp. curry powder
dash of hot pepper sauce (page 96)
1 tsp. minced cilantro
salt and fresh-ground black pepper

Divide the vegetables in half and place in 2 bowls or on sheets of waxed paper. Place the garlic, chicken, and half the vegetables in a Dutch oven or stockpot. Add water to cover the chicken, then the basil, curry powder, hot pepper sauce, cilantro and salt and pepper to taste. Bring to a boil, then immediately reduce heat and simmer uncovered for about 2 hours.

Skim the fat off the top of the stockpot and strain the soup. Refrigerate the cooked chicken for later use.

Add the remaining vegetables to the soup. Simmer for another 10 minutes, or until the vegetables are tender, and serve.

FISH AND SEAFOOD

CONTENTS

CALYPSO COD STEAKS

SERVES 6

These cod steaks have zip, thanks to the hot peppers. Salmon works well, too, but do not use salted cod in this dish. Serve with any of the corn dishes in the section on Side Dishes.

3 tbsp. fresh lime juice
2 tbsp. olive oil
2 tsp. minced garlic
1 tsp. minced hot pepper or
2 tsp. hot pepper sauce (page 96)
6 cod or salmon steaks, ¾ inch thick and
weighing about 6 oz. each

In a bowl, whisk together the lime juice, olive oil. garlic, and hot pepper or hot pepper sauce.

Brush the broiler rack with oil and preheat the broiler. Broil the steaks for about 10–12 minutes on one side, basting frequently with the sauce, then turn and cook on the other side for another 10–12 minutes, again basting frequently, until done.

GRILLED SHRIMP POCKETS WITH
MANGO-PAPAYA CHUTNEY

SERVES 4

This is a lively dish that is great to serve at parties or barbecues where guests may eat standing up. The shrimp have a succulent taste from being cooked in their shells.

1 lb. medium shrimp in their shells, patted dry
1 tsp. vegetable oil
½ tsp. salt
4 × 6 inch pita bread pockets
1½ cups Mango-Papaya Chutney (page 102)
lime wedges, to garnish

Prepare the barbecue or heat the oil in a large cast-iron skillet over moderately high heat.

Toss the shrimp with some oil and spread in a single layer on a piece of heavy-duty aluminum foil or on a fine-mesh grill dish or basket and transfer to the grill. (If using foil, make certain it doesn't entirely cover the grill so that the smoke from the fire can reach the shrimp.) Grill the shrimp for about 2 minutes or until just pink around the sides. Turn with tongs and cook for another 2 minutes, until opaque when cut in the thickest part. If cooking on the stove, spread the shrimp in the skillet in a single layer and cook for 2 minutes, until opaque when cut in the thickest part.

Allow the shrimp to cool, then shell and discard the shells. Slice the shrimp in half lengthwise. Stir the sliced shrimp into ½ cup chutney.

Partially slit open each pita pocket and fill with the shrimp and chutney mixture. Serve immediately, garnished with the remaining chutney and lime wedges.

STEAMED RED SNAPPER WITH
ORANGE-CURRY SAUCE

SERVES 4

If snapper is not available, substitute any firm-fleshed lean fish, such as grouper, halibut, haddock, flounder, perch, turbot, or sole. I like to serve this with steamed vegetables or Twice-Cooked Fried Green Plantains (page 115). Guests like to dip their plantains as well as the fish into the Orange-Curry Sauce, and a dollop of sauce atop, say, steamed cauliflower is heavenly.

Orange-Curry Sauce
1/2 cup sour cream
4 tbsp. grated orange rind
2 tbsp. chopped fresh cilantro
1/4 tsp. onion powder
1/4 tsp. dry mustard
1/4 tsp. curry powder

Fish
3 whole allspice berries
1 1/2 lbs. red snapper, cross-sectioned into 4 steaks

Combine the sour cream, orange rind, cilantro, onion powder, mustard, and curry powder in a small bowl, and chill. Lightly grease a vegetable steaming rack and place it in a Dutch oven. Add water to just below the steaming rack and bring it to a boil. Toss the allspice berries into the boiling water and place the fish on the rack. Cover, reduce the heat, and simmer for 8–10 minutes or until the fish flakes easily when tested with a fork. Serve with the sauce.

BAHAMIAN GRILLED LOBSTER TAIL
SERVES 4

This is my version of an elegant dish served at the Runaway Hill Club in the Bahamas.

4 lobster tails (about 1½ lbs. in total), thawed if frozen, removed from shells intact and deveined
4 tsp. fresh lime or lemon juice
4 cloves garlic, minced
⅓ cup ghee or unsalted butter
1 cup dry breadcrumbs
2 tsp. salt
1 tsp. fresh-ground black pepper
½ tsp. dried thyme, crumbled
½ tsp. dried marjoram, crumbled
½ tsp. dried oregano, crumbled
½ tsp. dried basil, crumbled
½ tsp. dried rosemary, crumbled
½ tsp. dried sage, crumbled
½ tsp. garlic powder
¼ tsp. minced hot pepper or hot pepper sauce (page 96)
2 tbsp. fresh-grated Parmesan
vegetable oil

Rinse the lobster shells and dry with paper towels, then sprinkle them with lime or lemon juice. In a small saucepan, cook the garlic in ghee or butter over moderate heat for about 1 minute. Remove the pan from the heat.

In a shallow bowl, stir together the breadcrumbs, salt, pepper, thyme, marjoram, oregano, basil, rosemary, sage, garlic powder, hot pepper or hot pepper sauce, and Parmesan cheese. Roll the pieces of lobster meat in the garlic butter, dredge them in the breadcrumb mixture and return them to their shells.

Brush the grill with oil. Prepare the grill according to the manufacturer's directions. Grill the tails, shell sides down, on a rack set 4–6 inches over the coals, for 10 minutes, turning them occasionally from side to side. Cover the grill and grill tails for 5–10 minutes more or until they are just cooked through.

SHRIMP TAMARINDO
SERVES 4

Here's another yummy shrimp dish with a quite unusual flavor, thanks to the tamarind it contains. Add a crisp salad and serve on steamed rice.

2 tbsp. butter or margarine
2 tbsp. minced onion
1 clove garlic, crushed
1 green bell pepper, cored, seeded and chopped
2 tbsp. tomato paste
¼ cup sherry
1 bay leaf
½ cup tamarind juice (page 17)
2 tbsp. clear honey
¼ tsp. ground allspice
¼ tsp. salt
⅛ tsp. hot pepper sauce (page 96)
1 lb. medium shrimp, shelled and deveined
1 tbsp. fresh lime or lemon juice

Heat the butter in a large skillet. Add the onion, garlic, and green pepper, and sauté until tender. Add the tomato paste, sherry, bay leaf, tamarind juice, honey, allspice, and salt, stirring constantly until heated through. Reduce the heat and simmer, uncovered, until slightly thickened, about 5 minutes. Add hot pepper sauce to taste. Add the shrimp and stir until pink, 3–5 minutes. Remove the bay leaf and stir in the lime or lemon juice.

Prawn Tamarindo

CARIBBEAN RED SNAPPER

SERVES 4

Here's another treatment of one of the Caribbean's most delectable fishes. You'll be surprised how the mélange of spices and tomatoes permeates the fish with West Indian flavors. Serve with fluffy rice to soak up some of the juices. You can substitute any firm, white-fleshed fish such as perch, turbot, sole, grouper, halibut, haddock, or flounder for the snapper.

vegetable oil
1 medium onion, sliced
1 large tomato, peeled and chopped
1/2 tsp. ground allspice
1/4 tsp. dried oregano
1/4 tsp. dried thyme
1 tsp. chopped fresh cilantro, or to taste
1/2 bay leaf
2 tbsp. water
1 tsp. hot pepper sauce (page 96)
1 lb. red snapper fillets
1/2 tbsp. lime or lemon juice

1 small clove garlic, minced
1/2 large onion, chopped
1/4 chopped red bell pepper
1/4 chopped green bell pepper
1/2 tbsp. olive oil
1/4 cup sliced almonds

Preheat the oven to 400°. Coat a 13 × 9 × 2 inch baking dish with vegetable oil. Arrange the sliced onion in the dish and add the tomato, allspice, oregano, thyme, cilantro and bay leaf. Combine the water and hot pepper sauce, and gently pour over the tomato mixture. Rub the fish fillets with lime or lemon juice and arrange in the dish.

Sauté the garlic, onion, and red and green peppers in olive oil for about 3 minutes. Spoon over the fish. Cover and bake in the oven for 40–45 minutes or until the fish flakes easily when tested with a fork. Remove the bay leaf and garnish with the almonds.

POACHED SALMON FILLETS WITH DILL-AND-GINGER VINAIGRETTE

SERVES 4

This recipe uses a cold water fish but gives it a Caribbean spice treatment. Serve with Creamy Garlic Mashed Potatoes (page 114) or a rice-and-beans dish.

4 × 6 oz. boneless salmon fillets with skin on
9 large sprigs fresh dill
1 bay leaf
4 whole cloves
salt
9 whole black peppercorns
2 tbsp. white wine vinegar
Dill-and-Ginger Vinaigrette
2 tbsp. Dijon-style mustard
1 tbsp. grated ginger root
2 tbsp. finely chopped shallot
1 tsp. finely chopped garlic
2 tbsp. tarragon vinegar
¼ cup diced canned pimentoes
salt and fresh-ground black pepper
½ cup olive oil

Prepare the vinaigrette by whisking the mustard, ginger, shallot, garlic, vinegar, pimentoes, and salt and pepper together in a bowl. Then add the olive oil in a slow stream, whisking rapidly until well blended. Set aside.

Place the salmon fillets in a shallow saucepan with enough water to cover. Add all but one dill sprig, the bay leaf, cloves, salt, peppercorns, and vinegar. Bring the water to a boil and simmer for 3–5 minutes. Do not overcook. Drain and serve with the vinaigrette, giving the vinaigrette a last-second whisking, if necessary. Float the reserved sprig of dill on top of the bowl of vinaigrette.

SHRIMP CREOLE

SERVES 4–6

The liquid in this version of Shrimp Creole is reduced until the sauce becomes quite thick and flavorful. The water chestnuts add a crunchy Oriental texture.

2 tbsp. vegetable oil
1 large onion, chopped
8 cloves garlic, minced
2 large celery stalks, finely chopped
4 medium tomatoes, chopped
2 medium green bell peppers, chopped
2 tbsp. tomato paste
1 tsp. hot pepper sauce (page 96)
½ tsp. dried oregano
1 tsp. dried thyme
2 tsp. Worcestershire sauce
6 cups chicken stock
1½ lbs. large shrimp, shelled and deveined
8 oz. can sliced water chestnuts,
drained and rinsed or 8 oz. jicama, sliced
½ tbsp. lime juice

salt and fresh-ground black pepper
4 cups cooked white long-grain rice
1 tbsp. minced cilantro or parsley to garnish

Heat the oil in a large saucepan, skillet, or wok. Add the onion, garlic, celery, tomatoes, and peppers, and sauté over moderate heat until tender. Then add the tomato paste, hot pepper sauce, oregano, and thyme, and blend, stirring constantly, for about 2 minutes. Add the Worcestershire sauce and chicken stock, and bring to a boil over medium-high heat until thickened, about 30 minutes. Add the shrimp and water chestnuts, and simmer, uncovered, until the shrimp are opaque throughout, about 4 minutes. Remove from the heat and adjust the seasoning with more hot pepper sauce to taste, lime juice, and salt and pepper. Serve over or under a scoop of rice on warm dishes and sprinkle the top with cilantro or parsley. Serve immediately.

⟲
BROILED BACON-WRAPPED JUMBO SHRIMP WITH TWO TOPPERS
SERVES 4

1 tsp. chopped garlic
2 tsp. chopped shallot
½ cup good-quality olive oil
½ tsp. dried oregano
½ tsp. dried thyme
½ tsp. dried basil
salt and fresh-ground black pepper
16 jumbo shrimp, shelled and deveined but with tails
left on
8 slices lean bacon

Remoulade
2 egg yolks
2 whole eggs
2 tsp. Dijon-style mustard
juice of 1 lime
2 cups olive oil
2 tsp. horseradish sauce
1 tsp. paprika, sweet or hot according to taste
2 tsp. white wine vinegar
2 hard-cooked eggs, finely chopped
¼ cup finely chopped red onion
2 tsp. finely chopped capers
1 tsp. finely chopped hot pepper or hot pepper sauce
salt and fresh-ground black pepper
2 tbsp. chopped fresh cilantro

Curry Mustard
2 tbsp. ghee or butter
½ tsp. curry powder
1 tbsp. plus 1 tsp. honey
2 tsp. lime or lemon juice
2 tsp. Dijon-style mustard

To garnish
lime slices or cilantro sprigs (optional)

Combine the garlic, shallot, olive oil, oregano, thyme, basil, and salt and pepper in a bowl. Add the shrimp. Cover and allow the shrimp to marinate overnight in the refrigerator.

Preheat oven to 350°. Cook the bacon on a rack over a baking pan or broiler pan for 4–6 minutes. Wrap each shrimp tightly in bacon, using ½ slice per shrimp. Hold in place with a toothpick and refrigerate until ready to cook.

To make the Remoulade, place the egg yolks and whole eggs in a blender or food processor, and blend. Add the mustard and lime juice. With the motor running, add the oil in a thin stream until mayonnaise consistency is reached. Transfer the mixture to a bowl and stir in the horseradish, paprika, vinegar, hard-cooked eggs, onion, capers, hot peppers, salt and pepper, and cilantro and chill in the refrigerator for about 30 minutes.

To make the Curry Mustard, warm the ghee or butter in a small saucepan over a moderate heat. Turn the heat to high and cook the curry powder until it dissolves, 1–1½ minutes, stirring once. Stir in the honey, lime or lemon juice, and mustard.

Cook the shrimp under a medium-hot broiler until the bacon is crisp and the shrimp are cooked through, about 3 minutes each side. Transfer to a serving platter and garnish with a dollop of Remoulade or Curry Mustard. Garnish with lime slices and/or cilantro.

⟲
CURRIED BAKED ROUGHY
SERVES 4

Roughy is a mild-flavored, usually inexpensive, lean white fish that lends itself to many assertive sauces. If you can't find roughy, use red snapper, perch, turbot, sole, grouper, halibut, haddock, or flounder. If you are concerned about cholesterol levels, substitute a low-fat mayonnaise in this recipe.

vegetable oil
4 × 4 oz. orange roughy fillets
½ cup mayonnaise
2 tbsp. dry white wine
2 tbsp. lime or lemon juice
1 tsp. dried dillweed
1 tsp. curry powder

Preheat the oven to 350°. Brush a broiling rack with vegetable oil. Place the rack in a shallow baking pan and arrange the fillets on the rack.

Combine the mayonnaise, wine, lime or lemon juice, dillweed, and curry powder in a bowl, and blend well. Spread the mixture evenly over the fillets. Bake in the oven for 25 minutes or until the fish flakes easily when tested with a fork.

POULTRY

GRILLED SPICY-MARMALADE TURKEY CUTLETS

SERVES 4

Canned pineapple slices may be substituted – use as many drained rings as you like – in this recipe, but if you're using fresh pineapple, save the crown and use it as a garnish in the center of your serving platter. This dish can be done on the barbecue or a broiler. Serve with a hot or cold rice dish and a salad.

1 medium pineapple, cut lengthwise into quarters
with rind on and then scored crosswise into
1 inch thick slices
1 orange, cut into ¹/₂ inch thick slices
1¹/₂ tbsp. light brown sugar
8 oz. marmalade
2 tbsp. finely chopped green onion
(white and green parts)
¹/₂ tsp. crushed garlic
¹/₂ tsp. hot pepper sauce (page 96)
¹/₄ tsp. grated ginger root
¹/₂ tbsp. Worcestershire sauce
¹/₂ tbsp. vegetable oil
salt and fresh-ground black pepper
4 turkey cutlets, about ¹/₂ inch thick

About 1 hour before serving, prepare the outdoor grill for barbecueing. Sprinkle the pineapple and orange slices with brown sugar.

In a small bowl, mix the marmalade, green onion, garlic, hot pepper sauce, ginger root, Worcestershire sauce, oil, and salt and pepper.

Arrange the turkey cutlets and fruit on the grill over medium heat. Cook for 5–7 minutes, brushing the turkey frequently with marmalade-spice mixture, and turning the turkey and fruit occasionally, until the turkey just loses its pink color throughout.

Alternatively, preheat the broiler. Prepare the marmalade mixture as above and arrange the fruit, with the pineapple flesh-side up, on a rack in a large broiling pan. Place the pan as close as possible to the heat and broil for about 5–7 minutes until the fruit is browned and bubbly. Remove and keep warm.

Arrange the turkey cutlets on the broiling pan. Place as close as possible to the heat and broil the turkey for 5–7 minutes, brushing frequently with marmalade-spice mixture and turning the cutlets once, until the turkey just loses its pink color throughout.

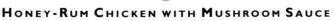

HONEY-RUM CHICKEN WITH MUSHROOM SAUCE

SERVES 4

Serve the sauce over the chicken and accompany with cooked vegetables, pasta or rice.

4 large chicken breasts, boned, skinned and fat cut off
¼ cup orange juice
1 tbsp. honey
1½ tbsp. clarified butter
2 cloves garlic, crushed
1 cup sliced button mushrooms
1 cup sliced oyster mushrooms
1 cup dark rum
2 cups chicken stock
salt and fresh-ground black pepper
½ cup light cream
2 eggs, beaten
2 tbsp. chopped fresh cilantro
orange slices, to garnish (optional)

Poke several holes in the chicken breasts with a knife point. Mix the orange juice and honey, and marinate the chicken in it for 20 minutes. In a large, heavy-based skillet, brown the chicken in 1 tbsp. clarified butter. Remove from the heat and set aside.

Melt the remaining butter in the same skillet, then add the garlic and mushrooms, and sauté for 1 minute. Pour in the rum and flame it. Add the chicken stock, salt and pepper, and chicken, and simmer over a low heat for 30 minutes. Just before serving, beat the cream with the eggs and add to the skillet. Cook over low heat for about 1 minute. Add the cilantro, check the seasoning and cook for a further 1 minute. Garnish with orange slices, if desired, and serve.

Stewed Chicken Trinidad-Style

STEWED CHICKEN TRINIDAD-STYLE

SERVES 4–6

2 tbsp. lime juice
1 medium onion, chopped
1 large tomato, cut into 8 wedges
1 celery stalk, chopped
1 tbsp. chopped green onion
3 tbsp. minced fresh cilantro
1 clove garlic, chopped
1/8 tsp. dried thyme, crumbled
1 tsp. salt
1/8 tsp. fresh-ground black pepper
1 tbsp. white wine vinegar
2 tbsp. Worcestershire sauce
1 1/2–2 lbs. chicken, cut into serving pieces
2 tbsp. vegetable oil
2 tbsp. firmly packed dark brown sugar
2 tbsp. ketchup
1 cup water
2 cups shredded cabbage (optional)

To garnish
celery leaves (optional)
lime slices (optional)

In a large bowl, combine the lime juice, onion, tomato, celery, green onion, cilantro, garlic, thyme, salt, pepper, vinegar, and Worcestershire sauce. Add the chicken, turning it to coat well, and leave it to marinate in the refrigerator, covered, overnight.

In a heavy kettle, heat the oil over medium-high heat until it is hot but not smoking, and add the sugar. When the sugar mixture begins to bubble, transfer the chicken in batches to the kettle, using a slotted spoon. Reserve the marinade mixture. Cook the chicken, turning it until it is browned well, and transfer it to paper towels to drain. Stir the reserved marinade mixture, ketchup, and water into the fat remaining in the kettle and return the chicken to the kettle. Bring the mixture to a boil and simmer it, covered, stirring occasionally, for 30 minutes. Add the shredded cabbage, if using, and simmer for 15–20 minutes until the thickest pieces of chicken are done. Garnish with celery leaves or lime slices if desired.

CARIBBEAN COCONUT CHICKEN

SERVES 4

4 chicken breasts, halved, boned, skinned
and fat cut off
2 tbsp. vegetable oil
1 large red bell pepper, cored, seeded and diced
1 large green bell pepper, cored, seeded and diced
1 large onion, chopped
1 clove garlic, crushed
3/4 cup unsweetened coconut flakes, toasted
2 tsp. grated lime rind
salt
2 tbsp. butter or margarine
1/4 tsp. sweet paprika
1/4 tsp. hot pepper sauce (page 96)
1 tbsp. lime juice
1 tbsp. apricot preserve
fresh cilantro, to garnish (optional)

Preheat the oven to 350°. Pound the chicken to 1/4 inch thickness between two sheets of plastic wrap and set aside. Heat the oil to medium hot in a large skillet and sauté the peppers, onion, and garlic for about 10 minutes, stirring frequently, until slightly soft. Remove from the heat. In the same skillet, stir in the coconut, lime rind, and salt to taste.

Spoon one-eighth of vegetable mixture over the center of each chicken breast. Bring the long ends of each breast up over the filling and secure with toothpick. Place the butter or margarine in a small roasting pan and melt over medium heat. Place the chicken rolls, seam-side down, in the pan. In a small bowl, combine the paprika, hot pepper sauce, and 1/2 tsp. salt, and sprinkle the mixture over the chicken rolls. Bake for 25–30 minutes until the chicken is cooked through and juices run clear when the roll is pierced with a knife. Remove the rolls to a chopping board.

Stir the lime juice and apricot preserve into the drippings in the roasting pan and bring to a boil, stirring to loosen browned bits on the bottom of the pan and to blend. Remove from the heat.

Remove the toothpicks from the chicken rolls and cut into 1/2 inch slices. Arrange the slices on a serving platter and pour the sauce over. Garnish with fresh cilantro if desired.

✺
FRIED CHICKEN CUBANO
SERVES 4–6

Cuban food is not hot but it is well seasoned and flavorful. If you would like to make this dish a little hotter – the way it is enjoyed in the Dominican Republic and Puerto Rico – chop up a small hot pepper and add it when you toss the reserved marinade into the pot.

6 large whole chicken legs with thighs,
or 4 large chicken breasts with wings attached
or detached
2 cloves garlic, finely chopped
³/₄ tsp. salt
¹/₄ tsp. fresh-ground black pepper
¹/₂ tsp. oregano
¹/₂ tsp. ground cumin
¹/₂ cup Seville orange juice or
¹/₄ cup orange juice and ¹/₄ cup lime juice
1 large onion, thinly sliced
¹/₄ cup vegetable oil

Arrange the chicken in a single layer in a large baking dish. Combine the garlic, salt, pepper, oregano, cumin, pepper, and orange juice. Mix well and spoon evenly over the chicken. Top with onion slices, cover and marinate for at least 2 hours or overnight in the refrigerator, turning the chicken occasionally. Remove the baking dish from the refrigerator 1 hour before cooking. Drain the chicken, reserving the marinade, and pat dry with paper towels.

In a large skillet, heat the vegetable oil over medium heat. Add the chicken and sauté until brown, about 5 minutes per side. Add the marinade and onions. Reduce the heat to low and cook for 25 minutes.

✺
SAUTÉED CHICKEN COMPOTE
SERVES 4

4 large chicken breasts, boned, skinned
and cut in ¹/₂ inch strips
¹/₂ cup curry powder
¹/₄ cup clarified butter
1 ripe papaya, peeled, seeded (seeds reserved)
and cut into ³/₄ inch chunks
2 bananas, sliced crosswise ¹/₄ inch thick
4 tbsp. unsweetened coconut flakes, toasted
¹/₂ cup dark rum
6 tbsp. coconut cream
¹/₂ tsp. salt
¹/₂ tsp. white pepper

Dredge the chicken strips in curry powder. Melt the clarified butter in a large skillet over high heat. Stir in the chicken and sauté until golden brown. Add the papaya, bananas, and coconut flakes. Add the rum, which will ignite, and let the alcohol burn off.

Add the cream of coconut and simmer until heated then season with salt and pepper. Stir quickly and serve immediately along with a chilled green salad topped with your favorite vinaigrette and sprinkled with papaya seeds.

SWEET SOUR 'N' HOT CHICKEN

SERVES 4

½ cup marmalade
½ cup lime juice
1 tsp. chopped ginger root
1 tsp. ground nutmeg
dash of hot pepper sauce (page 96)
1 tbsp. vegetable oil
4 large chicken breasts (about 1½ lbs.), boned,
skinned, fat cut off, cut into 1 inch cubes
1 medium papaya, seeded, halved
and cut into 1 inch cubes
6 oz. can sliced water chestnuts, drained
½ cup fresh cilantro, chopped

In a small saucepan, melt the marmalade over a low heat, gradually blending in the lime juice, ginger, nutmeg, and hot pepper sauce. Heat the oil in a skillet and brown the chicken cubes. Add the papaya and toss for several minutes, then add the sauce and water chestnuts. Cook over a moderate heat for about 3–4 minutes until the chicken is cooked through. Taste the sauce and add hot pepper sauce to taste. Spoon on to a serving dish and sprinkle with cilantro.

JERKED DISHES

CONTENTS

JERK MON'S CHICKEN

SERVES 4—6

This jerk dish incorporates a classic rub – a combination of spices, brown sugar, and hot peppers that is applied to the chicken to enliven the dish. About the only thing this granddaddy of rubs has in common with the others that follow is that the extremely hot *habañero* or Scotch Bonnet peppers are used.

*4 tsp. allspice berries, crushed in mortar and pestle,
or 1 tsp. ground allspice
6 cloves garlic, crushed
2 tbsp. peeled and chopped ginger root
2 tbsp. dark brown sugar
¼ cup yellow mustard
1 tsp. ground cinnamon
¼ cup hot peppers, stemmed, seeded and chopped
hot pepper sauce (page 96), to taste
½ cup olive oil
2 green onions, sliced
¼ cup cider vinegar
2 tbsp. lime juice
salt and fresh-ground black pepper
3–3½ lbs. chicken, jointed,
or 6 large whole legs, or 4 large breasts*

Purée the hot peppers in a blender or food processor. Add the allspice, garlic, ginger, sugar, mustard, cinnamon, hot pepper sauce, olive oil, green onion, vinegar, and lime juice, and blend until the mixture is a smooth paste. Add salt and pepper to taste and blend again.

Cut the chicken legs and thighs apart. Cut breasts in half crosswise, leaving the wings attached. Gently lift the skin up from the chicken, exposing the meat, and rub the paste underneath. Then rub into the outside of the skin. Cover with plastic wrap and refrigerate for 2 hours.

Barbecue or broil the chicken for about 40 minutes at low heat, turning once, until the skin is dark brown and crusty.

To cook on a covered barbecue, place the coals on one side and the chicken on the other. Cover and cook for 40–50 minutes.

To cook in the oven, preheat it to 350°. Bake the chicken for 50 minutes then transfer to the broiler and broil for 2–3 minutes on each side until the skin is dark brown and crusty.

MAKE AHEAD MOLASSES JERK

SERVES 4–6

Molasses, which is not as sweet as sugar, imparts a subtle, sweet nuance and lends a rich mahogany color to this dish. The jerking is all done below the skin and this makes this dish an ideal candidate for the sauce listed below. This chicken can also be made a day in advance, covered and refrigerated.

2½ tbsp. cider vinegar
1½ tbsp. Worcestershire sauce
¾ tbsp. molasses
¾ tbsp. grated ginger
¾ tsp. hot pepper sauce (page 96)
2 cloves garlic, finely chopped
1 medium onion, finely chopped
2 small green olives, sliced (optional)
¾ tsp. ground allspice
¾ tsp. ground cinnamon
¾ tsp. salt
¾ tsp. fresh-ground black pepper
3–3½ lbs. chicken, jointed,
or 6 large whole chicken legs, or 4 large breasts

Combine the vinegar, Worcestershire sauce, molasses, ginger, hot pepper sauce, garlic, onions, olives, allspice, cinnamon, salt, and pepper in a heavy-duty food storage bag. Shake to combine the marinade.

Gently pull the skin away from the chicken pieces without detaching it. Place the chicken pieces in the food storage bag and seal the bag, pushing out all of the air. Leave to marinate, refrigerated, for at least 2 hours or overnight.

Preheat the oven to 400°. Remove the chicken from the marinade and pull the skin back over the chicken. Discard the remaining marinade. Place the chicken in a single layer in a flame-proof dish. Bake in the oven for about 40 minutes or until the skin is crispy and juices run clear when the chicken is pierced with a fork. If making ahead, refrigerate the chicken. To reheat, bring the chicken to room temperature then bake at 375° for about 30 minutes, covered loosely with foil. If necessary, place the chicken under a hot broiler for 1 minute to crisp the skin.

The natural abundance of coconuts on the islands has led to the use of the milk and flesh in a wide variety of dishes and drinks.

SKINNY SKINLESS JERKED CHICKEN

SERVES 4

This dish leans toward sweet and spicy and is not hot at all. Serve with Pigeon Peas and Rice (page 117).

2 tbsp. chopped onions
4 tsp. fresh thyme or 1 tsp. dried
2 tsp. salt
2 tsp. ground nutmeg
4 tsp. sugar
2 tsp. fresh-ground black pepper
4 × 6 oz. chicken breasts, boned, skinned and fat cut off
1 tbsp. butter or margarine
1 tbsp. oil

Combine the onion, thyme, salt, nutmeg, sugar, and black pepper in a small bowl or in a food processor. Prick the chicken breasts several times with a knife point, place in a non-reactive bowl and rub the mixture over both sides of each breast. Cover and refrigerate for about 20 minutes.

Heat the butter or margarine and oil in a skillet that will accommodate the breasts in a single layer. Add the chicken and sauté gently on each side for 5–10 minutes, depending on thickness. The chicken is done when the juices run clear.

COL. BAJAN'S BREADED FRIED CHICKEN

SERVES 4

Bajans rub jerk seasoning into slits cut in boiled chicken and then the chicken is breaded and fried. In this recipe, however, I recommend baking or micro-waving the chicken first so you can use a leaner chicken than one intended for boiling.

4 chicken breasts
1/4 cup hot peppers, stemmed, seeded
and finely chopped
6 green onions, finely chopped (including tops)
3 cloves garlic, minced
2 tbsp. lime juice
2 tbsp. chopped fresh cilantro
1 tbsp. chopped fresh chives
1/2 tsp. ground cloves
1/4 tsp. thyme
1/4 tsp. marjoram
1/4 tsp. paprika
1/2 tsp. fresh-ground black pepper
1 egg
1 tbsp. soy sauce
1 tbsp. hot pepper sauce (page 96)
flour for dredging
3 cups dry breadcrumbs
vegetable oil for frying

Bake or microwave the chicken breasts until tender. If microwaving the chicken, cover with waxed paper and microwave at high temperature for 13–15 minutes or until the breasts are no longer pink, rearranging them at 5 minute intervals. If pre-baking, preheat the oven to 350°, brush the chicken parts with vegetable oil or clarified butter, place in a shallow baking pan and bake until tender, about 30 minutes. Set aside to cool.

Combine the hot peppers, green onions, garlic, lime juice, cilantro, chives, cloves, thyme, marjoram, paprika, and black pepper. Cut deep gashes in the chicken and fill with the mixture.

Beat together the egg, soy sauce, and hot pepper sauce. Lightly dust the chicken with the flour, dip in the egg mixture and roll in the breadcrumbs.

Heat the oil to 375° and fry the chicken until golden brown, about 4 minutes on each side. Drain on paper towels and serve.

MCJERK NUGGETS

SERVES 4

Serve this with a rice or pasta dish for a meal the children especially will love. I like to cut the cubes in quarters when cold and serve them in a Caesar salad instead of anchovies.

2 lbs. chicken thighs and/or breasts,
skinned and chopped into 2 inch cubes
3 tbsp. plus 1–2 tsp. any jerk seasoning on page 92,
or prepared jerk seasoning

Rinse and drain the chicken cubes and pat dry with paper towels. Place in a bowl and rub in the jerk seasoning. Place in a heavy-duty, sealable, plastic food storage bag or a non-reactive bowl, covered, and leave to marinate for at least 1 hour or overnight in the refrigerator.

Preheat the oven to 350°. Place the chicken pieces in a roasting pan and bake, covered, until chicken is done (about 45 minutes), turning the chicken halfway through the cooking time.

Just before removing the chicken from the oven, mix 1–2 tsp. of jerk seasoning with some of the juices in the pan and a small amount of water to thin the sauce if necessary. Spoon over the cooked chicken and serve.

QUICK JERK PORK CHOPS

SERVES 4

This dish can be whipped up in no time. In fact, if you marinate the chops overnight, all you have to do next day is throw them on the grill or under the broiler. The same rub can be used with lamb chops, chicken breasts, or rib steaks. Serve with tomato and cucumber salad and some coconut rice and you've got a real taste of the tropics.

1/4 cup hot peppers, stemmed, seeded and chopped
2 oz. fresh allspice berries or
3 tbsp. powdered allspice
3 tbsp. lime juice
2 tbsp. chopped green onion
1 tsp. hot pepper sauce (page 96)
1 tsp. ground cinnamon
1 tsp. ground nutmeg
4 center-cut pork chops

In a food processor or blender, purée the hot peppers, allspice, lime juice, green onion, hot pepper sauce, cinnamon, and nutmeg to make a thick paste. Rub the mixture into the chops and marinate, covered, in the refrigerator for 1 hour or longer.

Grill the chops over a hot charcoal fire or under a hot broiler until done. The seasonings will cause the chops to char on the outside.

PIQUANT PORK CHOPS WITH AVOCADO SAUCE
SERVES 4

1 cup beer
²⁄₃ cup fresh basil, minced
¼ cup fresh lime juice
2 tbsp. plus ¼ tsp. hot pepper sauce (page 96)
1½ tsp. dry mustard
½ tsp. any dry jerk seasoning (page 92) or salt
2 cloves garlic, minced
4 × 5 oz. lean center-cut loin pork chops,
½ inch thick, trimmed of fat
2 tbsp. plus 2 tsp. light brown sugar
2 tbsp. coarse-grained mustard
1 tbsp. plus ¼ tsp. cider vinegar
1½ tsp. molasses
vegetable oil

Sauce
1 ripe avocado, peeled, pitted and coarsely chopped
1 tbsp. lime juice
¾ tsp. chili powder
¼ tsp. minced garlic
½ tsp. salt
2 tbsp. mayonnaise

Combine the beer, basil, lime juice, 2 tbsp. hot pepper sauce, dry mustard, jerk seasoning or salt, and garlic in a large sealable plastic food storage bag. Add the chops, seal the bag and refrigerate for 8 hours, turning the bag occasionally.

Combine the brown sugar, mustard, vinegar, molasses, and remaining ¼ tsp. hot pepper sauce in a small saucepan and bring to a boil. Reduce the heat immediately and simmer, uncovered, for 2 minutes. Set aside.

Brush a grill rack with oil and place over medium-hot coals or under a medium-hot broiler. Remove the chops from the bag and discard the marinade. Place the chops on the rack and cook for 5 minutes. Turn the chops over and brush with brown sugar mixture. Cook for 5 minutes or to taste.

In a blender or food processor, purée the avocado with the lime juice, chili powder, garlic, salt, and mayonnaise until smooth.

PORK CREOLE
SERVES 4

This is a well-seasoned, succulent dish. If you have leftovers, freeze or refrigerate the meat and use in recipes in Salads (page 39) or Appetizers, Sandwiches, and Snacks (page 29) calling for cooked pork.

1 tbsp. any dry jerk seasoning (page 92)
or prepared jerk seasoning
1½–2 lbs. pork tenderloin, trimmed of fat
1½ cups chicken stock

Rub the seasoning all over the pork. Place on a plate, cover loosely with plastic wrap and allow to marinate in the refrigerator for 2–3 hours.

Preheat the oven to 350°. Oil a large skillet and place it over high heat for about 3 minutes. Add the pork and sear on all sides, then transfer it to a baking dish and add the stock. Roast in the oven, turning the meat occasionally and basting it with stock, for 25–30 minutes. The interior should be just pink. Cut into ½ inch slices and serve.

CURRIED PORK CHOPS WITH RICE PILAF

SERVES 4

This is a subtly seasoned jerk dish that complements the curried rice. Add a tossed salad for a meal that can be put together in less than half an hour.

1 cup long-grain white rice
2 tbsp. vegetable oil
1 cup raisins
½ tsp. ground cumin
½ tsp. salt
½ tsp. fresh-ground black pepper
1¼ cups chicken stock
¼ cup water
1½ tsp. curry powder
⅛ tsp. ground cinnamon
⅛ tsp. chili powder
8 very thin pork chops (2 lbs. in total)

Toast the rice in 1 tbsp. oil in a saucepan for 2–3 minutes until golden. Stir in the raisins, ¼ tsp. cumin, salt, and pepper. Cook for 1 minute. Add the stock and water. Simmer, covered, until the liquids are absorbed by the rice, about 15–20 minutes.

Meanwhile, combine the curry powder, remaining cumin, cinnamon, and chili powder. Rub on the chops.

Divide the remaining oil between two large skillets and heat to moderately hot. Divide the chops between the skillets and cook, covered, for 3 minutes on each side until cooked through. Alternatively, cook in two stages in one skillet, keeping the first batch of chops warm. Serve with the rice.

GINGERY PORK CHOPS
WITH CURRIED MANGO
SERVES 6

No plain-Jane pork chops these, this spicy-fruity main dish is best served with simpler side dishes, such as plain white rice or black bean dishes. A Creole Spinach Salad (see page 40) will add some contrasting color and texture.

6 center-cut loin pork chops, about 1 inch thick,
trimmed of fat
1½ tsp. grated ginger root or ground ginger
3 cloves garlic, crushed
½ cup dry sherry or dry wine
½ cup ginger marmalade or orange marmalade
¼ cup soy sauce
2 tbsp. light sesame oil

Curried Mango
2 mangoes, cut in bite-size chunks
(or canned unsweetened mango or 4 nectarines)
2 tbsp. butter or margarine, melted
¼ cup firmly packed brown sugar
1–1½ tsp. curry powder

Make the Curried Mango first. Preheat the oven to 350°. Place the drained mango in a pie plate. Combine the butter or margarine, sugar, and curry powder, and spoon over the fruit. Bake in the oven for 30 minutes. Keep warm until the pork chops are done.

With a knife point, make 6 incisions, less than ¼ inch deep, on each side of the chops. Make a paste of the ginger and garlic, and rub it into the meat on both sides, spreading any remaining paste on top of the chops. Set aside.

Combine the sherry or wine, marmalade, soy sauce, and sesame oil. Mix well and pour over the chops. Shortly before serving time, prepare the barbecue. Place a drip pan under the grill rack. Place the chops on the hottest part of the grill and cook, covered, for about 15 minutes, basting occasionally with the sauce and turning 2 or 3 times. Alternatively, cook uncovered in the oven at 350°.

🌀
JERK BURGER
SERVES 4

Everyone loves a burger and your favorite jerk seasoning will give lean chuck steak a boost in flavor. Serve on lightly toasted hamburger buns with a variety of condiments, plus plates of lettuce leaves, sliced onions, and ripe tomatoes.

2 lbs. lean chuck steak, ground
1/2 tbsp. any dry jerk seasoning (page 92)
or prepared jerk seasoning
dash of hot pepper sauce (page 96)
1 tsp. sugar
1 small onion, chopped
1 1/2–2 tbsp. dry breadcrumbs
vegetable oil

Blend the meat, jerk seasoning, hot pepper sauce, sugar, onion, and breadcrumbs together in a large bowl. Form into burgers and cook on a lightly oiled grill or skillet, turning once, until done. If you like, sprinkle an extra coating of dry jerk seasoning on the burgers before you flip them over to make a charred crust.

🌀
RUB-A-DUB FISH FRY
SERVES 4–6

In the broadest sense, seafood and fish are also jerked whenever they are combined with spices and hot peppers, such as in Conch Scotch Bonnet Fritters (page 34). But here's a recipe in which the jerk seasonings are used in the traditional jerk manner – as a rub. While flying fish is used in this Bajan recipe, fillets of any white firm-fleshed fish may be substituted – for example red snapper, perch, turbot, or sole.

6 flying fish or any white fish fillets
1 small onion, finely chopped
salt
white pepper
dash of aromatic bitters
1 clove garlic, finely minced
sprig of fresh thyme, finely chopped
sprig of fresh marjoram, finely chopped
vegetable oil
1 tbsp. dark rum
1 egg
breadcrumbs

Rinse the fish fillets and dry with paper towels. Combine the onion, salt, white pepper, bitters, garlic, thyme, and marjoram. Rub the mixture firmly into the fillets on both sides.

In a skillet large enough to hold all the fillets (or use two skillets), heat the oil to medium-hot. Beat the rum and egg together. Dip each fillet into the egg, then coat with breadcrumbs. Fry for 2–3 minutes on each side until the fish is opaque.

Jerk Burgers

SIX EASY DRY JERK BLENDS

Once you've tasted some of the recipes in this chapter you may want to try some other combinations. The first four are very simple and use exclusively dry seasonings. The last two incorporate some fresh ingredients, but only the final recipe – Rum Jerk – calls for ingredients to be added at the last minute when you're ready to jerk your dish. Each dry recipe makes a small amount – about ⅓ cup. When you find one you especially like, make a batch and store it in a tightly sealed jar in the refrigerator. These jerk blends can be rubbed into just about any meat, fish or seafood, or used in salads and soups to add pizzazz. The dry ones also make nifty seasoning blends to sprinkle on boniato chips and fried green plantains. I like to brush croutons with olive oil and then shake them in a paper bag with dry jerk seasoning to coat.

1 THREE KINDS OF FIRE

2 tsp. chili powder
1½ tsp. ground cumin
½ tsp. cayenne pepper
2 tsp. salt

2 FOUR PEPPERS PLUS

1 tbsp. sweet paprika
1 tsp. onion powder
1 tsp. garlic powder
1 tsp. cayenne pepper
½ tsp. ground black pepper
½ tsp. ground white pepper
½ tsp. ground cumin
dash of salt

3 MELANGE

1¼ tbsp. sweet paprika
1 tbsp. garlic powder
1 tbsp. ground black pepper
½ tbsp. chili powder
½ tbsp. dried thyme
½ tbsp. dried oregano
½ tbsp. onion powder

4 EAST-WEST INDIES

3 tsp. curry powder
3 tsp. sweet paprika
1½ tsp. ground cumin
¾ tsp. ground allspice
½ tsp. chili powder

5 EASY BAJAN

1 medium onion, chopped
1 clove garlic, minced
3 green onions, chopped, including some green tops
about ½ inch square of hot pepper, chopped
1 tsp. minced fresh cilantro
1 tsp. minced thyme
sprig of marjoram
¼ tsp. allspice
½ tsp. salt
fresh-ground black pepper
dash of Worcestershire sauce

6 RUM JERK

2 tbsp. garlic powder
2 tsp. ground ginger
2 tsp. ground allspice
½ tsp. ground cinnamon
½ tsp. ground nutmeg
2 tsp. salt
3 bay leaves, crumbled
2 tsp. cayenne pepper
½ cup lime juice
1 medium onion, sliced
1 cup dark rum
½ cup brown sugar

Combine the garlic powder, ginger, allspice, cinnamon, nutmeg, salt, bay leaves, and cayenne pepper, and store in a tightly covered jar in the refrigerator. When ready to jerk, combine this mixture with the lime juice, onion, rum, and sugar. Give the meat at least 2 hours in the marinade in the refrigerator, and use it frequently during grilling or broiling as a baste.

TWO SASSY SAUCES

HOT SWEET 'N' SOUR SAUCE
MAKES ABOUT 2 CUPS

This makes an intriguingly tropical accompaniment to all jerked dishes as well as other poultry, pork, or game dishes. The sauce will keep for about 6 weeks in a refrigerated, tightly sealed container.

2 tbsp. vegetable oil
1 medium onion, roughly chopped
3 ripe bananas (about 1 lb.), sliced ½ inch thick
¾ cup guava nectar
¼ cup fresh orange juice
1 tbsp. dark brown sugar
1½ tsp. curry powder
1 tbsp. white vinegar
2 tbsp. lime juice
salt and fresh-ground black pepper

In a medium non-reactive saucepan, heat the oil over moderate heat. Add the onion and cook until softened, 5–7 minutes. Add the bananas and cook, stirring frequently, for about 5 minutes. Add the guava nectar, orange juice, sugar, curry powder, and ½ tbsp. vinegar. Bring to a boil over high heat. Reduce the heat and simmer gently until the mixture thickens to the consistency of apple sauce, about 10 minutes.

Remove from the heat and stir in the remaining vinegar and the lime juice. Season with salt and pepper to taste. Serve hot or at room temperature.

Fruits are used on a wide scale, both as an ingredient and as a garnish.

TART TAMARIND SAUCE
MAKES ABOUT 1½ CUPS

This palate-teasing sauce is a lovely counterpoint to hot jerked dishes or to roasted pork and veal.

2 cups tamarind juice (page 17)
2 oz. dried tamarind pulp
2 cups chicken stock
¼ cup dry sherry
1 tsp. cornstarch
1 tbsp. cold water

In a medium saucepan, combine the tamarind juice and pulp over medium heat. Reduce to a simmer and cook, stirring occasionally, for 20 minutes. Add the stock and sherry, and cook for 25 minutes more. Strain the sauce, discarding the pulp.

Mix the cornstarch in the cold water. Add to the tamarind mixture and stir. The sauce should be the consistency of apple butter.

MEATS

CRISPED PORK CHUNKS WITH HOT PEPPER SAUCES

SERVES 4–6

These tasty morsels are called *griots* in Haiti, *masas de puerco* in Cuba, and are related to the dish called garlic pork in Trinidad. The marinade renders the chunks tender inside, and browning them after simmering gives them a delicious crusty coating similar to meats grilled over an open fire. Serve with your choice of sauces (page 96) and/or prepared Caribbean hot sauces. (When you discover your favorite, make it in a larger batch to use in any recipe in this book that calls for hot pepper sauce.) As accompaniments to this spicy dish, I prefer a salad of well-chilled greens and a cold soup or bean salad.

3 lbs. pork tenderloin, cut into 1 inch chunks
1 large onion, finely chopped
½ tsp. dried thyme
1 cup Seville orange juice or
½ cup orange juice and ½ cup lime juice
1 fresh hot pepper, chopped
2 cloves garlic, minced
½ cup peanut oil
fresh-ground black pepper to taste
salt to taste
¼ tsp. ground cinnamon
½ tsp. ground cumin

In a glass dish or bowl, mix the pork chunks with the onion, thyme, orange juice, hot pepper, garlic, pepper, salt, and spices. Cover and refrigerate for 6–8 hours. Transfer to a large heavy-based skillet or saucepan, add cold water to cover the meat and cook over medium heat until the liquid begins to boil. Reduce the heat and simmer for about 1 hour or until the meat is cooked throughout.

Drain the meat and pat dry with paper towels. Heat the oil in a skillet and fry the meat quickly, turning each piece over as it is browned. Serve immediately.

HOT HOT HOT PEPPER SAUCE

MAKES ABOUT 2 CUPS

1 cup vinegar
6 tbsp. lime or lemon juice
2 onions, finely chopped
6 radishes, finely chopped
2 cloves garlic, crushed
2 tbsp. stemmed, seeded and finely chopped hot pepper
4 tbsp. olive oil
fresh-ground black pepper and salt to taste

Mix everything in a non-reactive bowl and serve. Store leftover sauce in a tightly sealed glass jar.

PAPAYA HOT PEPPER SAUCE

MAKES ABOUT 2 CUPS

2 tbsp. stemmed, seeded and finely chopped
hot peppers
½ cup chopped papaya
½ cup raisins
1 cup finely chopped onion
3 cloves garlic, minced
½ tsp. turmeric
¼ cup malt vinegar

Combine all the ingredients in a non-reactive saucepan and bring to a boil, stirring constantly. Reduce the heat and cook for 5 minutes. Put the mixture in a blender or food processor, purée until smooth and serve. Store leftover sauce in a tightly sealed glass jar.

LIME-HORSERADISH SAUCE

MAKES ABOUT 2 CUPS

⅓ cup grated horseradish
⅓ cup lime juice
⅓ cup prepared mayonnaise
½ cup plain yogurt
salt and fresh-ground black pepper

Blend all the ingredients in a blender or food processor in a non-reactive mixing bowl for 1 minute, or by hand until thoroughly blended. Chill (and store) in a tightly sealed glass jar overnight to allow flavors to blend completely.

⊚

HOT MARMALADE SAUCE

½ cup lime or orange marmalade
6 oz. grated horseradish

Mix the horseradish into the marmalade by the spoonful, tasting as you go. Chill (and store) in a tightly sealed glass jar.

⊚

GINGER PORK CUBES WITH
LIME-HORSERADISH SAUCE

SERVES 8–10

Pork roasts are so versatile in Creole cooking. Leftover pork from this dish can be used to make a number of other recipes in this chapter and the chapter on Jerked Dishes. I like to refrigerate the leftover cooked chunks in the marinade for Crisped Pork Chunks with Hot Pepper Sauces (page 96).

1½ lbs. lean boneless pork, cut into 1 inch cubes
3 tbsp. soy sauce
1 small clove garlic, crushed
½ tsp. fresh-ground black pepper
½ tsp. sugar

1 tsp. minced ginger root
1 tsp. peanut oil
Lime-Horseradish Sauce (page 96)

Mix the pork with the other ingredients. Place in a glass bowl, cover and leave to stand for 2 hours, turning the meat several times.

Preheat the oven to 325°. Spread the pork in a single layer in a baking pan and bake for 1 hour, turning several times during cooking. Serve with Lime-Horseradish Sauce.

ROAST PORK PUERTO RICAN-STYLE

SERVES 8–10

Here's an enticing treatment of an economical cut: leg of pork. This is a favorite dish in Puerto Rico, where it is known as Fabada Asturiana, and the Puerto Rican love for assertive, spicy flavors is amply demonstrated in this recipe. There are plenty of ways you can use leftover pork, too – see recipes in this chapter and in Jerked Dishes. In this recipe, adjust the amount of onions and squash according to how many you wish to serve.

1 tbsp. minced garlic
3 tbsp. olive oil
½ tsp. dried oregano leaves, finely crumbled
¾ tsp. ground cumin
1 tsp. salt
½ tsp. black pepper
1 cup chopped green onions
1 cup chopped fresh cilantro
1 cup chopped green bell pepper
1 cup white rum
1 leg of pork (about 7 lbs. with bone)
2 × 8 oz. baking potatoes, scrubbed,
each cut lengthwise into 8 wedges
1–3 large red onions, each cut into 8
2–4 pieces squash, such as Hubbard or butternut, or
calabaza, peeled and cut into 1 inch slices (optional)
2–4 yellow summer squash or zucchini cut into
1 inch slices (optional)

Gravy
4 tbsp. fat from drippings in roasting pan
4 tbsp. all-purpose flour
½ tsp. black pepper
4 cups water or beef stock

Sauté the garlic in the olive oil until tender. In a blender or food processor, blend the olive oil-garlic mixture with the oregano, cumin, salt, pepper, green onions, cilantro, green pepper, and rum to make a paste.

Place the meat in a non-reactive baking pan slightly larger than the meat. With a long, sharp knife, score the top of the roast in a diamond pattern, cutting through the rind and underlying fat almost to the meat. Rub the seasoning paste into the roast, cover, and marinate in the refrigerator overnight.

Heat the oven to 325°. Unwrap the meat and roast it for 2 hours. Add the potatoes, onions, and squash, if using, to the roasting pan and brush with drippings. Roast for 1 hour, then add the squash, or zucchini, if using, and brush with drippings. Continue to roast for another 45 minutes (the meat should roast for a total of 32–35 minutes per 1 lb.) or until a meat thermometer inserted in the thickest part (not touching the bone) registers 185° and the vegetables are tender.

Remove the meat to a chopping board and cover loosely with foil (reserve the pan drippings for gravy). Leave to stand for 15 minutes before slicing. Arrange the vegetables on a platter and cover to keep warm.

If you are planning to reserve some of the meat and pan gravy for other meals, proceed as follows: slice one-third of the pork and serve with the vegetables, reserving 1 cup pan juices for gravy. Then slice half the remaining pork thinly (about 1 lb.) and wrap tightly in heavy freezer wrap. Shred the remaining meat (about 12 oz.), cover and refrigerate. Sliced pork will keep for 2 weeks in the freezer; shredded about 1 week in the refrigerator.

To make the gravy, pour the fat into a medium saucepan and sprinkle the flour into it. Whisk over medium-high heat until smooth, scraping up browned bits. Gradually whisk in the water or beef stock until blended. Bring to a boil, reduce the heat and simmer for 5 minutes or until thickened, stirring 2 or 3 times. Cool and refrigerate about half the gravy in a tightly sealed container if you are planning to use it in another meal.

GARLICKY PORK LOIN TAMARINDO
SERVES 10–12

Here is another cut of pork that will render multiple meals, for example Tropical Pork Salad (page 51). A sauce that tastes good with this dish is Orange-Curry Sauce (page 65).

6 lbs. center-cut pork loin, boned, rolled and tied
8 medium cloves garlic, 2 halved, 6 crushed
2 tsp. salt
1½ tsp. grated lemon rind
1 tbsp. fresh thyme leaves or 1 tsp. dried, crumbled
1 tbsp. fresh oregano leaves or 1 tsp. dried, crumbled
½ tbsp. fresh cilantro
¼ cup peanut oil
1 tbsp. Worcestershire sauce
1 tbsp. gin
2 tsp. brown sugar
1 cup tamarind juice (page 17)
3 bay leaves

To garnish
tomato slices (optional)
bell pepper slices (optional)

Make four deep cuts over the surface of the pork and insert the garlic halves. In a blender or food processor purée the crushed garlic, 1 tsp. salt, 1 tsp. lemon rind, thyme, oregano, and cilantro to make a thick paste. Press the mixture into the opening of the rolled roast with a spoon.

In a small mixing bowl, combine the oil, Worcestershire sauce, gin, sugar, and remaining salt and lemon rind. Rub this mixture vigorously into the surface of the pork. Place the roast in a large non-reactive bowl. Soak the bay leaves in tamarind juice for a few minutes and then pour over roast. Cover and refrigerate for 24 hours, turning occasionally.

Bring the pork to room temperature. Preheat the oven to 300°. Drain any liquid from the roast and place it on a rack in a roasting pan. Cover with foil and roast for 30 minutes. Increase the temperature to 350° and roast for 1¼ hours, uncovered.

Prepare the barbecue. Grill the pork until the surface is golden and crusty, turning occasionally (about 50 minutes). Transfer the pork to a serving platter, cover with foil and leave to stand for 20 minutes. (The pork can also finish cooking in the oven – roast for about 1¼ hours longer.)

If you are planning to use part of this pork for additional meals, slice and store according to the instructions in Roast Pork Puerto Rican-Style (page 98). To serve for this meal, slice the pork thinly. Garnish with slices of tomato and/or pepper if you wish and serve at room temperature.

GINGER RUM-GLAZED HAM
SERVES 8–10

I like to make this dish for holidays and serve it with a chilled rosé wine – the slight sweetness of the wine marries well with the subtle sweetness of the ham. You'll want to try this glaze on precooked ham slices too for a quick, delicious meal.

7–8 lbs. half (shank end) fully cooked cured ham
2 tbsp. grated ginger root
3 tbsp. firmly packed brown sugar
3 tbsp. dark rum
cilantro sprigs, to garnish (optional)

Preheat the oven to 350°. If the ham still has the skin attached remove most of it with a sharp knife, leaving a layer of fat and a collar of skin around the bone. Trim the fat, leaving a layer about ¼ inch thick, and score the layer remaining into diamonds. Bake the ham on a rack in a roasting pan for 55 minutes.

In a blender, blend together the ginger, sugar, and rum. Spread this glaze over the ham and bake for 30–35 minutes more, or until the glaze is brown and bubbly. Transfer the ham to a serving platter, garnish with cilantro if desired, and leave to stand for 15 minutes before carving.

PORK CHOPS PIÑA
SERVES 4

¹/₂ cup pineapple juice
¹/₄ cup dry white wine
1¹/₂ tbsp. olive oil
¹/₄ tsp. salt
¹/₈ tsp. fresh-ground black pepper
4 × 3 oz. boneless pork loin chops
¹/₂ cup chopped onion
¹/₂ small hot pepper, seeded and minced
3 medium tomatoes, blanched, peeled,
seeded and chopped
2 tbsp. chopped fresh cilantro
³/₄ tsp. ground cinnamon
¹/₄ tsp. ground nutmeg

To prepare the marinade, combine the pineapple juice, wine, half the oil, salt, and black pepper in a very large sealable plastic food storage bag. Add the pork chops, seal the bag, squeezing out the air, and turn to coat the chops. Refrigerate for at least 2 hours or overnight, turning the bag over occasionally.

To prepare the sauce, heat the remaining oil in a small saucepan. Add the onion and pepper, and cook, stirring frequently, for 5 minutes, until tender. Add the remaining ingredients and simmer for 3 minutes. Drain the marinade into the sauce, bring to a boil and simmer for 10 minutes longer. Meanwhile, broil the chops or grill 5 inches from the coals of a barbecue for 7 minutes on each side, until cooked through but still juicy. Serve each chop with an equal amount of the sauce.

🌀

CITRUSY PORK FILLET WITH
MANGO-PAPAYA CHUTNEY
SERVES 4–6

1/2 cup fresh orange juice
1 tbsp. fresh lime juice
1 1/2 tsp. sugar
1/2 tsp. salt
1/4 tsp. ground allspice
pinch of ground nutmeg
1 tsp. grated ginger root
3 cloves garlic, minced
8 oz. pork tenderloin
vegetable oil
1/2 tsp. light brown sugar

Mango-Papaya Chutney
1 ripe mango or 4 oz. canned unsweetened
mango, cut into bite-sized chunks
1 ripe papaya or 2 nectarines or 3 oz. canned
unsweetened papaya, cut into bite-sized chunks
1 tbsp. chopped green onions
1 tbsp. fresh lime juice
1 tbsp. chopped fresh cilantro
1 tsp. chopped hot pepper or hot pepper sauce

Combine the orange juice, lime juice, sugar, salt, allspice, nutmeg, ginger, and garlic in a large sealable plastic food storage bag. Add the pork, seal the bag, and marinate in the refrigerator for 8 hours, turning occasionally.

Preheat the oven to 350°. Remove the pork from the bag, reserving the marinade. Place the pork on a rack brushed with oil. Place the rack in a shallow roasting pan and pour hot water and half the reserved marinade into the roasting pan to a depth of 1/2 inch. Insert a meat thermometer into the thickest part of the pork. Bake for 40 minutes, or until the meat thermometer registers 160°, basting frequently with the remaining marinade mixed with light brown sugar.

While the meat is cooking, combine the mango, papaya, green onions, lime juice, cilantro, and hot pepper or hot pepper sauce. Chill and serve with the pork.

STEWED LAMB SINT MAARTEN
SERVES 4–6

Traditionally, this dish from the Netherlands Antilles is made with goat. This lamb version is even more delicious. I like to serve it with rice, mashed potatoes or noodles, and a minted vegetable.

2 tbsp. vegetable oil
2 lbs. boneless lamb, cut into 2 inch cubes
2 medium onions, chopped
4 cloves garlic, chopped
½ cup chopped celery
1 tsp. finely chopped ginger root
3 tbsp. minced **habañero** *peppers or hot pepper sauce*
(page 96)
1 small green bell pepper, chopped
2 medium tomatoes, peeled and chopped
1 tbsp. lime or lemon juice
1 tsp. ground cumin
1 tsp. ground allspice

½–¾ cup beer
1 tbsp. red wine vinegar
1 large cucumber, peeled and chopped
¼ cup pitted green olives (optional)
1 tbsp. capers (optional)

Heat the vegetable oil in a Dutch oven over medium-high heat. Brown the lamb in the oil, then remove and drain. Add the onions, garlic, celery, ginger, hot peppers or hot pepper sauce, and green pepper, and sauté until the onions are soft.

Combine the lamb, onion mixture, tomatoes, lime or lemon juice, cumin, and allspice, and cover with beer. Simmer until the meat is very tender and starts to fall apart, about 1½ hours. Add more beer if necessary.

Add the vinegar, cucumber, and olives and capers if using, and simmer for 15 minutes before serving.

PEPPERPOT STEW

SERVES 6—8

This dish is said to come from Amerindian cuisine and is still eaten on many islands, including Tobago, Saint Kitts, and Barbados. It seems a pepperpot is always simmering on the stove in the islands – some West Indians joke that great-great-great grandmother started their pot going some decades ago.

2 tbsp. chopped hot peppers or hot pepper sauce
(page 96)
2½ lbs. chicken, cut into serving pieces
1 oxtail
1 lb. lean pork or beef, cut into 1½–2 inch cubes
2 tbsp. vegetable oil
1 large onion, cut into wedges
3 tbsp. brown sugar
1 tsp. ground allspice
1 tsp. thyme
2 tsp. ground cinnamon
1 tsp. ground cloves
2 tbsp. malt vinegar

Place the chicken in a stock pot and cover with water. Bring to a boil, reduce the heat and simmer for 45 minutes, skimming off any scum. Remove the chicken and reserve the broth in the stock pot. Remove the chicken meat from the bone and chop.

In a large skillet, brown the oxtail and pork or beef in oil. Drain the meat on paper towels. Add the onion wedges to the skillet and sauté until soft.

Combine the chicken, oxtail, pork or beef, onions, and broth in the stock pot. Stir in the sugar, allspice, thyme, cinnamon, and cloves, and simmer for 1 hour until the meat is tender and the stew is thick. Stir in the vinegar and serve.

SIRLOIN STEAK WITH PINEAPPLE CHUTNEY

SERVES 4—6

2–2¼ lbs. sirloin steak, cut 1½ inches thick
and trimmed of fat
3 tbsp. vegetable oil
½ tsp. salt
¼ tsp. fresh-ground black pepper
1 tsp. curry powder
¼ tsp. garlic powder
¼ tsp. ground ginger
½ tsp. allspice
dash of nutmeg
dash of cinnamon

Pineapple Chutney
20 oz. can crushed pineapple, drained
¼ cup finely chopped green onion,
including some green top
¼ cup flaked coconut, preferably unsweetened
⅓ cup finely chopped red bell pepper
1 tbsp. hot pepper sauce (page 96)
1 tbsp. grated ginger root
1 tbsp. fresh lime juice
1 tbsp. dark rum
salt and white pepper

Brush both sides of the steak with vegetable oil. In a small bowl, mix the salt, pepper, curry powder, garlic, ginger, allspice, nutmeg, and cinnamon. Transfer the mixture to a large sheet of waxed paper and roll both sides of the steak in it, patting the mixture into the surface. Set aside.

To make the chutney, combine the pineapple, green onion, coconut, red pepper, hot pepper sauce, ginger, lime juice, rum, and salt and pepper in a non-reactive bowl and toss gently. Cover and leave to stand at room temperature until ready to serve.

To cook the steak, place a large, heavy-based skillet over medium-high heat and add the remaining oil. When hot, add the steak and cook for 4 minutes on each side or to taste.

Alternatively, to barbecue: brush the grill rack with vegetable oil and place 5–6 inches from the coals. Grill the steak over glowing coals for about 8 minutes on each side for medium rare steaks. Transfer to a serving platter and serve.

Sirloin Steak with Pineapple Chutney

SIDE DISHES

CONTENTS

HOPPIN' JOHN

SERVES 4

This dish is undoubtedly African in origin. No one quite knows how it got its name, but each cook seems to have his or her own recipe for this mixture of rice and black-eyed peas. Folklore holds that eating it on New Year's Day brings good luck, probably because the dish is so filling you won't want for much more. Unfortunately, it also brings fat and cholesterol when cooked in the traditional manner with ham hocks, hog jowls or bacon. This adaptation will, I hope, bring good nutrition as well as luck. If you wish to make a vegetarian version, just skip the meat altogether.

3 cups water
2 chicken bouillon cubes
1 medium ripe tomato, chopped
10 green onions, chopped

1 bay leaf
1 tsp. dried thyme
1 tsp. hot pepper sauce (page 96)
1¹/₃ cups long-grain white rice
16 oz. can black-eyed peas, drained and rinsed
6 oz. cooked ham, trimmed of fat and cut in bite-sized cubes
salt and fresh-ground black pepper

Bring the water, bouillon cubes, tomato, green onions, bay leaf, thyme, and hot pepper sauce to a boil in a large kettle. Add the rice, cover, and simmer until tender, about 25 minutes. Stir in the black-eyed peas and ham, cover, and simmer for 8–10 minutes.

SWEETER-THAN-SWEET SWEET POTATOES

SERVES 4

Bring a taste of the tropics to your table in no time with this simple dish. It's wonderful with ham or pork chops, and with its bright color you won't need a garnish.

4 large sweet potatoes, boiled and sliced
2 × 8 oz. cans crushed pineapple, drained
1/2 tsp. ground nutmeg

2 tsp. grated ginger root
2 tsp. ground cinnamon
2 tbsp. dark rum

Preheat the oven to 350°. Layer the sweet potatoes in an ovenproof dish. Combine the pineapple, nutmeg, ginger, cinnamon, and rum, and pour over the potatoes. Bake for 5 minutes and serve.

PAIN PATATE

SERVES 4

This aromatic Haitian dish is a sweet potato pudding using boniatos, the white-fleshed tropical tuber with a scent like that of violets. If you cannot find boniatos in your area, substitute ordinary white potatoes and add 1 tsp. allspice to the dish.

1¹/₂ cups boniato, grated
1¹/₂ cups evaporated milk
1 cup coconut milk (page 94)
3 very ripe bananas, mashed
1 cup firmly packed brown sugar
1 egg

¹/₂ tsp. ground cinnamon
¹/₂ tsp. ground nutmeg
1 tsp. vanilla extract
¹/₂ tbsp. dark rum
2 tbsp. unsalted butter, melted
grated rind of ¹/₂ lime

Preheat the oven to 400°. Mix together the boniato and evaporated milk, coconut milk, bananas, sugar, egg, spices, rum, butter, and lime rind. Pour into a buttered baking dish and bake for about 1 hour. Serve warm or cool.

CURRIED CORN-VEGGIE MELANGE
Serves 4

2 tbsp. butter
3 tbsp. chopped green onions
1 tsp. minced garlic
2 tsp. curry powder
4 ears fresh sweetcorn, kernels scraped from cobs
1 red bell pepper, cut into thin 1½ inch long strips
2 green bell peppers, cut into thin 1½ inch long strips
4 small ripe plum tomatoes, cut into ½ inch cubes
½ cup finely diced cucumber
½ cup finely diced jicama (optional)
salt to taste
2 tbsp. chopped fresh cilantro
2 tbsp. coconut milk (page 14) (optional)
hot pepper sauce (page 96), to taste

Heat the butter in a skillet. Add the green onions, garlic, and curry powder, and cook, stirring, until the onion is soft. Add the corn, peppers, tomatoes, cucumber, jicama (if using), and salt. Blend well, cover, and cook over medium heat for about 2 minutes. Add the cilantro, coconut milk (if using), and hot pepper sauce, blend well and serve.

CALYPSO RICE
Serves 4

This is an everything-but-the-kitchen-sink dish that magically blends many flavors and textures. Instead of chicken, I frequently substitute lean pork or beef.

1 cup long-grain white rice
1 tsp. salt
2 oz. baby corn
½ cup whole button mushrooms, straw mushrooms or your own choice, coarsely chopped
¼ cup coarsely chopped water chestnuts
1 carrot, coarsely chopped
1 tbsp. coarsely chopped fresh cilantro or parsley
1 medium onion, coarsely chopped
½ medium red bell pepper, coarsely chopped
½ medium green bell pepper, coarsely chopped
¼ cup butter or margarine
1½ tsp. soy sauce

½ chicken breast (about 4 oz.), cooked and coarsely chopped
⅔ cup frozen green peas

Preheat the oven to 325°. Boil the rice in salted water until tender but firm. Drain and set aside in a deep pan. Sauté the baby corn, mushrooms, water chestnuts, carrots, cilantro or parsley, onion, and peppers in the butter or margarine until tender. Set aside.

Mix the soy sauce and chicken into the warm rice. Blend in the vegetables, transfer to a 1 quart casserole and bake for 15–20 minutes. Cook the peas just before removing the casserole from the oven. Drain the liquid from the peas, mix into the casserole and serve.

CREOLE POTATOES
SERVES 4

8 small new potatoes (about 1 lb.),
peeled (optional) and quartered
³/₄ tsp. any dry jerk seasoning (page 92)
1 tbsp. butter or margarine, melted
2 tbsp. chopped fresh cilantro
cilantro sprigs, to garnish (optional)

Place the potatoes in a steamer rack over boiling water. Cover and steam for 12–15 minutes or until tender. Transfer the potatoes to a bowl and sprinkle with jerk seasoning. Add the butter and cilantro, and toss to coat the potatoes thoroughly. Garnish with cilantro sprigs, if desired.

COCO-LOCO BEANS 'N' RICE
SERVES 4

In traditional Caribbean cooking coconut milk is frequently combined with black-eyed peas, but in this adaptation red kidney beans benefit from this rich treatment as well. Jamaicans make a version of this colorful dish called Jamaican Coat of Arms. This adaptation, though, also borrows from Haitian cuisine with the addition of pungent mushrooms.

2 cups water
1¹/₂ oz. dried Haitian black mushrooms, porcini,
or German pfifferlinge, coarsely broken up and
presoaked in hot water for 30 minutes (optional)
2 cups coconut milk (page 14)
8 oz. can red kidney beans, rinsed
1 tsp. malt vinegar
1 tsp. dried thyme
3 whole peppercorns, ground
2 whole allspice berries, ground
1 cup long-grain white rice
1 small onion, coarsely chopped

1 clove garlic, crushed
vegetable oil for frying
¹/₄ cup drained and coarsely chopped cooked bacon
1 tsp. salt for cooking rice
salt and fresh-ground black pepper to taste

In a non-reactive medium saucepan, bring the water, mushrooms, and coconut milk to a boil, skimming the surface. Add the beans, vinegar, thyme, peppercorns, and allspice. Reduce the heat, cover and simmer for 10 minutes. Stir in the rice with a fork. Reduce the heat to low, cover, and cook until the rice is tender, for about 20 minutes.

In the meantime, fry the onion and garlic in a small amount of vegetable oil until tender and add to the rice-and-beans mixture, along with the chopped bacon. Bring to a simmer, cover and cook for 10 minutes. Fluff the mixture, with a fork, adding salt and pepper to taste and serve.

YUCA-CHIVE PANCAKES
SERVES 4

The mild oniony flavor of chives gives a needed flavor boost to this otherwise bland tuber. These make tasty accompaniments to any main dish. I like to serve them with a dollop of Lime-Horseradish Sauce (page 96) or a small dish of Papaya Hot Pepper Sauce (page 96).

1 lb. fresh yuca, peeled
2 tbsp. chopped fresh chives
1 egg, beaten
salt and fresh-ground black pepper
½ cup dry breadcrumbs
6 tbsp. butter

Boil the yuca until it can be easily pierced with a fork, about 35–45 minutes. Drain well. When cool enough to handle, remove any stringy sections and discard. Cut the yuca into 1 inch thick sections and purée in a blender or food processor. Press through a coarse sieve into a bowl. Stir in the chives, then the egg, then salt and pepper. Form into 3 inch patties about ½ inch thick. Place the breadcrumbs in a small bowl. Turn each pattie in the breadcrumbs to coat, shaking off excess.

Melt the butter in a heavy-based medium skillet over medium-high heat. Add the patties and cook for 5 minutes on each side until golden brown. Remove from the skillet with a slotted spoon and drain on paper towels. Serve immediately.

CREAMY GARLIC MASHED POTATOES

SERVES 4

2–3 large baking potatoes (about 1 lb.), scrubbed
4 cloves garlic, unpeeled
salt and fresh-ground black pepper
¹/₂ cup milk
1 tbsp. butter
¹/₄ tsp. ground nutmeg
1 small egg, beaten
2 tbsp. Cheddar cheese, grated

Place the potatoes and garlic cloves in a large saucepan and cover with cold salted water. Bring to a boil over high heat, then cover and reduce the heat to moderate. Simmer until the potatoes are tender, about 45 minutes. Drain the potatoes and garlic, peel the potatoes and squeeze the garlic cloves from their skins. Return the potatoes and garlic to the pan, and mash them.

Preheat the broiler. Heat the milk in another saucepan. Add the butter and nutmeg to the milk, and stir until the butter melts. Add the milk gradually to the potatoes, stirring with a wooden spoon. Add the egg and blend well, then add salt and pepper to taste.

Transfer the mixture to a 9 inch gratin dish or baking pan. Smooth the top with a spatula and sprinkle with cheese. Place under the broiler until nicely browned.

TWICE-COOKED FRIED GREEN PLANTAINS WITH WARM CURRY SAUCE

SERVES 4

You can jazz this dish up for a party by topping with sour cream and caviar, the Warm Curry Sauce below or Orange-Curry Sauce (page 65).

2 cups vegetable oil
2 green plantains (1 lb.), peeled and sliced into
¹/₂ inch rounds
salt and white pepper

Warm Curry Sauce
1 cup water
¹/₂ cup instant non-fat milk powder
1 ¹/₂ tbsp. all-purpose flour
¹/₄ tsp. salt
pinch of white pepper
2 tsp. clarified butter
¹/₂ tsp. curry powder

First, prepare the curry sauce: combine the water, milk powder, and flour in a heavy saucepan. Stir until smooth. Cook over medium heat, stirring constantly, until the mixture is thickened and bubbly. Stir in the remaining ingredients.

In a medium saucepan, heat the oil until hot but not smoking, about 375°. Fry the plantain rounds 4 at a time in the hot oil until well browned (2–3 minutes), keeping the oil hot. Drain on paper towels.

Using a rolling pin or two wooden chopping boards, squash the fried plantains into flat rounds.

Refry the plantain rounds, 6–8 at a time, until golden brown all over, about 2 minutes. Drain on paper towels. Season with salt and pepper, and serve hot or at room temperature with the sauce.

MALANGA-GARLIC PANCAKES

SERVES 4

Get out of the potatoes-or-rice rut with this nutty-tasting tropical tuber. If you can't find malanga, substitute zucchini. These pancakes are especially good with roast beef, steaks, roast pork, and strongly flavored fish.

1 ¹/₂ lbs. malanga, coarsely grated
1 tbsp. chopped garlic
1 tbsp. chopped green onion
salt and fresh-ground black pepper
1 egg, lightly beaten
3 tbsp. all-purpose flour
¹/₄ cup vegetable oil

Combine the malanga, garlic, green onion, and salt and pepper. Add the beaten egg and stir in lightly. Stir in the flour.

Heat the oil in a deep, heavy-based, large skillet. For each pancake, drop 1 heaped tbsp. mixture into the pan and flatten slightly with the back of a spoon. Fry over medium heat for 2–3 minutes on each side, or until golden brown. (Turn very carefully so the oil doesn't splatter.) Drain on paper towels. Stir the mixture before frying each new batch.

TROPICAL TUBER FRIES WITH CURRIED MAYO DIP

SERVES 4–6

1 egg white
1 tbsp. dry jerk seasoning (page 92)
1¼ lb. yuca, boniato or malanga,
cut into very thin ½ inch wide sections
vegetable oil
salt

Curried Mayo Dip

⅔ cup mayonnaise
⅓ cup plain yogurt
1 tbsp. curry powder
1 tsp. ground ginger
½ tsp. turmeric powder
½ tsp. paprika, preferably sweet Hungarian
½ tsp. chili powder
¼ tsp. salt

In a small bowl, stir together the mayonnaise and yogurt. Stir in the spices and ¼ tsp. salt, cover and refrigerate for at least 1 hour or overnight.

Preheat the oven to 400°. In a large bowl, lightly beat the egg white with a fork until foamy. Stir in the dry jerk powder. Add the tuber slices and toss to coat.

Place the tuber slices on non-stick baking sheets and drizzle with oil, tossing to coat. Spread in a single layer and season lightly with salt. Bake for 30–40 minutes. Serve with the curry dip.

BLACK BEANS LATINO

SERVES 6–8

If you have leftovers of this basic bean dish, purée some of the bean mixture in a little of the bean liquid and add hot pepper sauce and dry jerk seasonings to taste to make a bean dip. You might also try tossing in some sliced black olives, raisins, and slivered almonds for a sweet and nutty note.

1 lb. dried black beans, rinsed and picked over
9 cups cold water
2 small ham hocks (about 1¼ lbs.)
½ cup plus 2 tsp. olive oil
2 large onions, finely chopped
4 cloves garlic, finely chopped
1 large green bell pepper, finely chopped
½ tsp. ground cumin
½ tsp. ground oregano
2 bay leaves
salt
2 tsp. hot pepper sauce (page 96)
1 tbsp. red wine vinegar
1 tsp. sugar
chopped onion, to garnish (optional)

Presoak the beans, if necessary, according to directions on the package. Drain them and place in a large pot with the water and ham hocks. Bring to a boil and cook slowly, uncovered, skimming the surface as necessary to remove any scum. The beans should be tender in about 1½ hours.

Meanwhile, heat the oil in a skillet and add the onion, garlic, and green pepper. Cook, stirring, until the onion is translucent and the peppers are tender. Add the cumin and oregano, and stir well.

After the beans have cooked for about 1 hour, transfer the onion mixture to the bean pot along with the bay leaves and hot pepper sauce. When the beans are tender remove the bay leaves and ham hocks. Season with hot pepper sauce, salt, vinegar, sugar, and 2 tsp. olive oil. This dish may be prepared one day in advance and reheated.

Serve the beans on a bed of rice and offer chopped onion separately to be sprinkled on top of the beans. Place a cruet of olive oil and one of hot pepper vinegar on the table for guests to add to the dish to their taste.

PIGEON PEAS AND RICE

SERVES 4

This dish is eaten on many of the islands. In the Bahamas it's called, appropriately enough, Bahamian Pigeon Peas and Rice. In Puerto Rico, it's called arroz con gandules – or the same minus the "Bahamian". If you can't find pigeon peas, substitute red beans, preferably small red kidney beans. This dish is great with chicken or any meat, and can make a one-dish meal if leftover bits of meat are added.

2 tbsp. oil
1 small onion, chopped
2 cloves garlic, crushed
4 tbsp. tomato paste
2 ripe tomatoes, chopped
1 green bell pepper, chopped
1/2 tsp. thyme

4 tbsp. chopped fresh cilantro
16 oz. can pigeon peas, drained
1 cup long-grain white rice
2 cups water
2 tbsp. fresh lime juice
hot pepper sauce (page 96) to taste
salt and fresh-ground black pepper to taste

Heat the oil in a saucepan and add the onion. Cook gently for 5 minutes then add the garlic and tomato paste, chopped ripe tomatoes, green bell peppers, and thyme. Cook for another minute. Add the cilantro, pigeon peas, and rice, and sauté for 1 minute. Add the water and lime juice, and cook gently, covered, for 15 minutes until the rice is cooked. Add hot pepper sauce, salt and pepper to taste, and serve.

BREADS AND DESSERTS

BREAD PUDDING WITH RUM SAUCE

SERVES 4

Bread Pudding
1 cup milk
¹/₂ cup heavy cream, plus extra for serving
¹/₄ cup sugar
2 small egg yolks
1 large egg
¹/₂ tbsp. vanilla extract
¹/₂ tsp. ground nutmeg
pinch of salt
8 slices (each ¹/₂ inch thick) fresh banana bread,
Coconut Bread (page 122) or any special bread of
your choice
1¹/₂ large bananas, cut into ¹/₄ inch thick rounds

Rum Sauce
4 tbsp. unsalted butter
3 tbsp. dark brown sugar
2 tbsp. freshly squeezed lemon juice
¹/₂ cup rum
¹/₄ cup water

Generously butter a 3 quart ovenproof baking dish. Whisk the milk, cream, and sugar together in a large bowl. Add egg yolks and whole egg one at a time, whisking well after each addition. Whisk in the vanilla, nutmeg, and salt, and set aside.

Cut 7 slices of bread into fingers 1 inch wide. Arrange an even layer of bread fingers on the bottom of the dish, cutting and fitting them to cover the bottom, and curve slightly up the sides of the dish. Cover with an even layer of banana slices and then pour enough custard over to cover them. Repeat the layers of bread and bananas.

Cut the remaining slice of bread into cubes and sprinkle over the bananas. Pour the rest of the custard over the top, press down lightly on the bread cubes and cover. Set aside for 30 minutes.

Meanwhile, preheat oven to 350°. Bake the pudding until it is almost solid through, about 45 minutes. Then remove the cover and bake until the cubes of bread on top are golden, an additional 15 minutes. Remove and set on a wire rack to cool.

While it is cooling, make the sauce. Melt the butter in a small saucepan over medium heat. Whisk in the sugar, lemon juice, rum, and water and bring to a rolling boil. Cook, whisking occasionally, until the mixture begins to thicken and the sugar has dissolved, about 5 minutes. Remove the sauce from the heat and transfer to a serving pitcher. Serve with the slightly cooled bread pudding and extra cream, if desired.

"BAKES"

These are the Creole version of a biscuit, fried in hot oil, and variations of this recipe are eaten throughout the islands. Make a big batch – they go fast!

2 cups all-purpose flour
2 tbsp. butter
½ tsp. salt
2 tsp. baking powder
2 tsp. sugar
⅔ cup milk

Sift the dry ingredients into a bowl, then cut in the butter with a knife until the mixture resembles breadcrumbs. Pour in the milk and stir to make a soft dough. Knead on a floured board for about 5 minutes, then refrigerate for 30 minutes. Break the dough into lemon-sized pieces, roll into balls and flatten to ½ inch thickness. Fry these in hot oil until golden.

COCONUT BREAD

MAKES 4 LOAVES

This is so nice for breakfast or tea with any jam, jelly, or marmalade – or spread a little cream cheese on a slice and *then* top with jam or marmalade! Slice a couple of the extra loaves thickly, wrap, and freeze, and you'll have a ready supply to pop in the toaster. These will keep for a couple of months.

1 lb. butter, softened
2 cups sugar
8 eggs
8 tsp. coconut extract
4 cups sour cream
1 lb. shredded coconut
8 cups all-purpose flour
4 tsp. baking soda
4 tsp. baking powder

Preheat the oven to 350°. Cream together the butter and sugar. Beat in the eggs and coconut extract, then the sour cream. Add the coconut. Stir together the flour, baking soda, and baking powder, and beat into a batter. Divide between 4 lightly greased loaf pans and bake for about 45 minutes, or until a toothpick inserted in the center comes out without any clinging batter or wet crumbs. Leave to cool before turning out.

PIÑA COLADA FRENCH TOAST

SERVES 4

Here's a holiday breakfast idea, although this dish is also elegant enough to serve as a dessert. Make Rum Sauce (page 120) to spoon over the toasts. Serve with steaming hot chocolate and Jamaican Blue Mountain coffee.

6 eggs
1 tsp. ground cinnamon
½ tsp. ground allspice
½ tsp. ground nutmeg
2 tbsp. dark rum
1 cup crushed pineapple, well drained
4–6 slices Coconut Bread
½ cup butter

Whisk the eggs, cinnamon, allspice, nutmeg, and rum together. Add the pineapple and whisk again. Put the bread in a large soup bowl or shallow dish, and pour the egg mixture over it. Turn the bread until it is completely saturated with the egg mixture. Fry in the butter until golden, and serve immediately.

BAKED BANANAS IN GUAVA SAUCE

SERVES 6

Fried bananas are a favorite in the Caribbean, but this recipe is a change from the ubiquitous caramelized brown sugar that usually goes into the dish. You can use different jam and fruit liqueurs to give the sauce a different flavor.

6 medium bananas, peeled, cut in half lengthwise
1 tbsp. dark brown sugar
2 tbsp. unsalted butter, cut into small bits
1/3 cup guava jelly or any seedless fruit jelly or jam
1 tbsp. fresh lime juice
1 tbsp. dry sherry

Preheat the oven to 350°. Place the banana halves cut side down in a 9 × 12 inch glass baking dish. Sprinkle the sugar evenly over the bananas and dot with the butter. Bake for 15 minutes.

Meanwhile, in a small non-reactive saucepan, combine the jelly or jam, lime juice, and sherry, and melt over low heat, stirring occasionally. Pour the jelly mixture over the bananas and bake for another 5 minutes. Place 2 banana halves on each plate and spoon some of the sauce on top. Serve immediately.

JAMAICAN COFFEE FLAN

SERVES 6

3/4 cup sugar
1/4 cup water
1 1/4 cups milk (do not use low-fat or non-fat)
1 cup whipping cream
2 tbsp. instant coffee powder
3 eggs
3 egg yolks
3/4 cup superfine sugar
3 tbsp. coffee liqueur

Place the oven rack in the center of the oven and preheat the oven to 325°. Place six 1/2 cup ramekins or soufflé dishes in a large baking pan. Place the pan in the oven and heat until the dishes are hot, about 10 minutes.

Meanwhile, bring the sugar and water to a boil in a small heavy-based saucepan, stirring until the sugar dissolves. Wash down any sugar crystals on the side of the pan with a wet pastry brush. Continue boiling, without stirring, until the mixture turns golden brown, about 10 minutes. Immediately divide the caramel mixture among the hot ramekins or soufflé dishes. Carefully tilt the ramekins or soufflé dishes to coat the sides with caramel mixture. Cool the dishes completely.

Bring the milk and cream to a boil in a heavy-based saucepan. Remove from the heat and stir in the instant coffee. Whisk the eggs and egg yolks together in a large bowl. Whisk in 1/4 cup superfine sugar and the coffee liqueur. Gradually whisk in the hot milk mixture. Strain the custard and divide among prepared ramekins or soufflé dishes.

Return the ramekins or soufflé dishes to the baking pan. Add enough simmering water to the baking pan to come halfway up the sides of the dishes. Bake until the edges are set and a toothpick pushed into the center comes out clean, about 50–60 minutes.

Remove the flans from the oven. Serve when cooled to room temperature in dishes. If making ahead of time, run a small sharp knife around the edges of the flans to loosen, refrigerate for 24 hours and, when ready to serve, invert on to plates.

MANGO FLAN

SERVES 6

This recipe combines two great Cuban loves: flan and mango. Canned pulp may be substituted for fresh, if you are making it out of season.

Caramel
¾ cup superfine sugar
1 tbsp. water

Flan
4 small eggs
2 egg yolks
½ cup sweetened condensed milk
½ cup milk
¼ cup plus 2 tsp. superfine sugar
8 oz. fresh mango pulp or nectarines or peaches,
puréed and strained

Mix the sugar and water in a small saucepan and cook on medium-high heat, stirring often, until the mixture bubbles and turns a light caramel color. Pour the caramel into 6 ramekins. Gently tilt the ramekins to coat the sides with caramel. Set aside to cool.

Preheat the oven to 250°. Add the eggs, egg yolks, condensed milk, milk, and sugar to the fruit pulp, and blend thoroughly. Pour into the caramelized ramekins. Place the ramekins in a large roasting pan and pour simmering water into the pan so it comes halfway up the sides of the ramekins. Bake for 40 minutes, or until a toothpick inserted in the center comes out clean. Chill before inverting to serve.

INDEX